DEAR MARCUS

a letter to the man who shot me

JERRY McGILL

SPIEGEL & GRAU   NEW YORK

2013 Spiegel & Grau Trade Paperback Edition

Published in the United States by Spiegel & Grau, an imprint of The Random House Publishing Group, a division of Random House, Inc., New York.

SPIEGEL & GRAU and Design is a registered trademark of Random House, Inc.

Originally published in hardcover in the United States by Spiegel & Grau, an imprint of The Random House Publishing Group, a division of Random House, Inc., in 2012.

Translation of "Du, Dunkelheit" by Rainer Maria Rilke is by Ernest Julius Mitchell II and is reprinted here by permission of the translator.

Photographs on pages 69 and 166 courtesy of Noreen McGill
Photograph on pages 138, 147, and 151 courtesy of the author
Photograph on page 140 courtesy of JoonMo Thomas Ku
Section-opening photos are courtesy of Chris Jones

Library of Congress Cataloging-in-Publication Data
McGill, Jerry.
Dear Marcus : a letter to the man who shot me / Jerry McGill.
p. cm.
ISBN 978-0-8129-8316-6—ISBN 978-0-679-64460-6 (ebook)
1. Children of single parents—United States—Biography. 2. Victims of violent crimes—United States—Biography. 3. Single-parent families—United States. I. Title
HQ777.4.M384 2012
306.85'60973—dc23   2011031251

Printed in the United States of America

www.spiegelandgrau.com

2 4 6 8 9 7 5 3 1

Book design by Liz Cosgrove

Friendships have been my life blood for as long as I can recall. If I were to reference every single person who has had a positive effect on me I could fill a chapter or four. I appreciate them all. But I must give a special shout out to my guys: Gil, Omid, Wind, and Marky Mark. And my dolls: Zora, Ariana, and Kirsten. Your unconditional support has made this moment possible.

You, darkness, out of whom I stem,
I love you more than the flame
that hems against the world
while sparkling
for a circle of some kind,
outside whose curve no being knows flame's shine.

Ah, but the darkness holds all in its fee:
figures and flames, beasts and me,
it grabs what it would,
humans and mights

And it can be that a great force could
be stirring in my neighborhood.

I believe in nights.

—Rainer Maria Rilke, "You, darkness, out of whom I stem"

author's note

All of my life, for as long as I can remember, I have been in love with the world of movies. For a kid who feared and despised his environment the cinema was the greatest form of escape. It started with watching *The Wizard of Oz* on a tiny TV set in my mother's bedroom and moved on to actually going to the cinema. I think the first film I actually saw on the big screen was *Grease*. From there I saw *Rocky, The Deer Hunter,* anything to get me out of the hood and into a fantastic world. As a child I would regularly attend movies on my own, usually sneaking into the theater. Often, in my darkest moments, I would envision my life as one long movie with a series of fade-ins, fade-outs, and dissolves. The film scenes depicted in this memoir are fictionalized accounts of the Movie of My Life.

Another thing: throughout this work I refer to the area

where I grew up as the Lower East Side. Today, due to massive gentrification, this area is currently known by many as the East Village. In my stubbornness, I will continue to call it the Lower East Side. At the time that I lived there, no one in their right mind would ever have thought of our neighborhood as part of the Village; it was truly that foreign and desolate.

Dear Marcus

INT. KITCHEN IN A TINY APARTMENT—DAY

EVELYN, late thirties, black, washes dishes while smoking a cigarette. A semipermanent scowl seems to be etched on her worn
face. DOREEN, baby-faced, sixteen, walks in and sits down at the
kitchen table. Across the screen reads the SUBTITLE: *MY MOM
REVEALS I'M ABOUT TO ENTER THE WORLD.*

                    EVELYN
          I'm a need you to go to the store.

                    DOREEN
          Okay.

                    EVELYN
          Two pack of Pall Malls, a dozen eggs. Money's
          on the dresser.

                    DOREEN
          Okay. Umm, Mama . . . can I ask you something?

                    EVELYN
          What is it, girl? I ain't got all afternoon.

                    DOREEN
          Mama . . . umm . . . I ain't had my period for near
          a week now.

After a beat Evelyn stops washing the dishes and turns to her daughter. Doreen stares down at the floor. Evelyn puts down her cigarette and dries her hands on her apron. She walks over to Doreen and smacks her hard across the face.

one

The idea to write to you was not an easy one, but I could no longer ignore the calling. It came swiftly and unexpectedly, like a thunderstorm on a humid afternoon or a tumor returned with a renewed ferocity. You can't keep a strong force down. The question becomes, why write to you now, some thirty years after the fact? Why bother to waste this precious blood, sweat, and energy on you—someone I never even met? Someone whom I can only imagine, but never truly visualize or come to understand? Why put any effort at all into contacting someone who came ever so close to ending my life with just the twitch of a finger? It's a valid question whose response is not very easy to articulate. But I suppose I have to try.

The scar from where the bullet entered my back is still there. It always will be, like a tattoo or stretch marks. I honestly never think about it now, as it is out of my sight line, but every so often it rises from the obscurity of my skin. At times a lover will be running her fingers down my neck in a caring, intimate manner and her finger will catch on that point. It feels like a zit now, no larger than a bee sting really. Still, the question always comes: "What's this from?"

The veracity of my answer will always depend on my feelings for the questioner. If I believe she will be around for a while, if she is someone whom I care enough about to share this darkness with, I will give just a little, but only so much.

"Oh, I was involved in an incident a while back," I'll say. You can't reveal too much too soon, you know. There's gotta be some mystery.

If it is someone I just leaned on for comfort at a particular moment, or someone I can tell is not truly "shareworthy," well, then she will receive the casual, harmless white lie. There will be no follow-up response. Not even eye contact. "Oh, that's nothing. Childish roughhousing," I will rattle off as if swatting away a fly. The majority have received the latter. I don't really like to share. It's not in my nature anymore. The events that occurred to produce that scar are not really a place I care to visit. As the saying goes, *I have moved on.* And I'm proud to make that statement. But now—in this moment in time—addressing *It,* addressing *You,* just feels appropriate. Until I speak to you, I can never fully close this door. And I need that resolution. I think I've earned it.

You—my nameless, faceless friend with whom I share such a close, personal relationship—do you ever think about me? Do you ever wonder what became of me—that kid whom you saw walking down the street that one brisk night in January? Was it your intention to link us indelibly with your simple, somewhat effortless act of violence? Were you even remotely aware of the potency of such an act? Did you blink? Give it a second thought? Did you say to yourself, *Maybe I shouldn't do this?*

I have created over a hundred scenarios for how we "met." With all my time in the hospital there was nothing to do but obsess. It was fascinating at first, putting together those shards of a jigsaw that would forever lack pieces. In my mind you are either black or Latino. Why? Simple deduction, since those are the only types of people who lived in that area where we grew up. I'm going to go ahead and make you black. I have the power now. You are positively a male since women don't typically go about ghettos shooting guns to prove their worthiness. Women don't really grow up with thuggish gun fantasies, do they? They sure as hell didn't back in 1982.

Maybe your name is Leroy. Or Tito. Or Dante. Or Hector. Or Tyrone. Or Javier. Or Jamal. Or Luis. For my own purposes, I have decided to give you a name. It helps me, you see, to give you a human character. You and I, we have such a poignant story and without a name for you the story is too difficult to convey. I am going to call you Marcus. Why Marcus? I don't know. That name speaks to me for reasons not fully apparent, and I believe in going with my first instinct. It fits. It just feels right. And so Marcus it is. Now tell me, Marcus, do you ever ask yourself, *What the fuck ever happened to that little dude that I shot in the back that one New Year's night? Did he die or what? Or maybe I just grazed him?*

We both know you didn't just graze me, because an ambulance came and we both know that an ambulance don't come to the hood unless something serious is going down. Perhaps you were watching as they took me away on a stretcher—sirens blaring, lights flashing, the whole deal. If you tried to follow up with me in the newspapers the next day you were out of luck, bro, because the shooting of a thirteen-year-old black kid on the Lower East Side? That doesn't make the newspaper in a city like New York.

Since our "meeting" I have lived in cities so tiny, so rural, that this type of event would have been the lead segment on the nightly news. But not here in New York. What with Sons of Sam, Bernard Goetzes, Mafia rubouts, and the occasional bludgeoning. Now if I had been a Kennedy or a Rockefeller or even a Cosby, well that's a whole other story. But no, I was just little Jerome. I didn't warrant so much as a byline.

So I'm just curious, always have been—why did you pick me, Marcus? You may recall that there were two of us walking that night. There was me and there was my best buddy, Eric. Same age, same height, same color. Did the fact that I was wearing a bright blue and silver Dallas Cowboys jacket have anything to do with it? Probably not. Were you high? Drunk? Strung out on crack? Were you and a friend screwing around taking pot shots out of your bedroom or living room window like me and Kahlil used to do with his BB gun, aiming at the pigeons on the roof across the street? Was I your pigeon?

Maybe you never really intended to shoot me? Maybe you meant to shoot near me and just scare us, not actually hit either of us. But hey, shit happens, right? Maybe you wrongly thought I was an old friend or an enemy: local drug dealer who recently dissed you. A guy you heard slept with your woman?

I have created so many scenarios in my head it is incredible. It's a wonderful gift having a creative mind. But sometimes it can be a curse as well. I have the powerful ability to fill in all the crevices and blank spots that you left behind. I get to touch up the masterful painting that you left undone so long ago. I am van Gogh and Matisse, Baldwin and Salinger, Dylan and Lennon. I will make my own reality and place you where I choose. This is my talent. My super power.

In my thoroughness I have conceived of just about every

possibility. Like the one that you, Marcus, are no longer even around anymore to read this. That perhaps, once you shot me and left me to die on that cold, hard pavement on Seventh Street and Avenue C, maybe something equally traumatic happened to you shortly thereafter. Maybe you went out to rob a grocery store and you were stabbed by the clerk behind the counter; left to die on a cold, uncaring checkered floor. Or maybe you were riding your bike that afternoon and you were hit by a taxi. Left to die in midtown traffic amid a crowd of hot dog vendors and tourists. Maybe you were busted later that week selling crack, went to Rikers, and got killed in the shower. Or in a prison riot. Or in the laundry room. Hey, maybe, just maybe, you were so riddled by guilt at realizing that you shot a helpless kid that you delved into a life of substance abuse and OD'd on heroin one cool February night. Left to die in a bathtub. Or you took a header off the roof of your building, not too far from where you shot me. Or you hung yourself in the broom closet of your day job as a junior high school janitor. I've thought of it all, over and over. It used to be all that I could do: come up with ways Marcus could die. Should die.

Truth be told, it doesn't really matter much because I didn't write this book for you, Marcus. My reasons for writing this are bigger than you or me, my friend. I wrote this book to release demons into the warm night air. I wrote this book to leave some scant history, a trail of breadcrumbs, for

the children I will never have and the children that you probably have had. I wrote this book so that someone else might
understand us. I wrote this book for any great number of
people who believe that Life really gave them the short and
shitty end of the stick. I wrote this book for all of those unfortunate suckers who were in the proverbial *wrong place at the
wrong time*. Were we chumps or what? Or were we?

Who knows, maybe in our own way we were actually the
lucky ones. Wouldn't that be a wondrous piece of irony,
huh? Perhaps, by virtue of circumstance and timing, we
avoided an even harsher reality. Cormac McCarthy wrote in
No Country for Old Men, "You never know what worse luck
your bad luck has saved you from." I love this perception.
Maybe, just maybe, it was our destiny to be in that so-called
wrong place at the wrong time. If that should be the case,
then I most likely owe you a debt of gratitude, Marcus old
boy. If you're still around, call me. I owe you a beer or two.

But I should reiterate, I didn't write this book for you,
Marcus. I wrote this for a certain population of the world:
Those who endure. Those who manage. Those who cope.
Those who get out of bed every morning and continue to go
on with the business of their lives *knowing what they know*.
Those who look into the eye of the storm and step out of it
battered, drenched, and unbeaten. Those who are determined to move on. Maybe you're one of us? Now that would
truly make for a great story, would it not?

I hope you are one of us, Marcus, because we all deserve a second chance; that shot at redemption. In many ways, we are probably very much alike, you and I. We were both given lemons. What did you do with yours, Marcus? I, for one, chose to make a martini.

INT. LIVING ROOM IN SMALL APARTMENT—DAY

JEROME, ten, sits on the couch, sad. DOREEN sits beside him. She puts her arm around his shoulder. SUBTITLE: *INTRO TO DEATH—VOLUME ONE*

DOREEN

You gonna be okay?

JEROME

Yeah. I'm gonna miss her. Why did she die?

DOREEN

I don't know. Maybe we kept the windows open too much and she got cold. Maybe we put too much vitamins in her water. I don't know, son.

JEROME

She was just getting used to me, you know? She would fly around and land on my shoulder or my head. I was gonna teach her to talk. It's not fair.

DOREEN

Life is not always fair, Jerome. Sometimes bad things happen to good people. That's just the way it is.

t w o

So I thought we could get a few things out of the way, Marcus. I wanted to share some of my history with you so that you might have a stronger understanding of the life you affected. I want you to know what I have learned—that all actions have consequences.

I wasn't originally from that neighborhood where we first met—the Lower East Side. No, I was actually from an even worse neighborhood if you can believe that. I was born in Brownsville, Brooklyn, and spent the first five years of my life there. One of the most infamous people to come out of this neighborhood: Mike Tyson.

I honestly don't remember much about that area or that part of my life, I was so young then, and nothing remarkable ever happened there. I have little bits of memories that feel more like dreams. Hanging outside on the stoop watching as a man was viciously attacked by a dog that another man had unleashed on him. Playing marbles in a filthy park. My mother, Doreen, barely twenty years old, making oatmeal on the stove in a tiny, roach-infested kitchen. It was a fire in our apartment that prompted us to move to Manhattan. We arrived via a crappy welfare hotel. There were just the three of us: my mother, my younger sister, Zonnie, and myself. Along the way there were a few pets—three birds, a cat, a hamster—but they never lasted long. One thing there never was? A father. I wonder, Marcus, if your experience was similar.

For me, our new neighborhood was a wonderful change. There seemed to be more light in Manhattan, and I don't just mean streetlights. It appeared to me that the sun was more favorable to Manhattan than it was to Brooklyn. The Brooklyn I remember was gray and full of shadows. In Manhattan, the way the projects were set up, they were all arranged in a kind of circle that allowed daylight more access to us. In Brooklyn, the buildings all seemed to stalk over you like great cement scarecrows, blocking out sunlight and optimism simultaneously. It was as if the Powers That Be were saying: *Such beauteous nature does not belong in such a dark and cold place as this Brooklyn.* Doesn't make sense, does it? I would think that that place needed it more than any I'd ever seen. But who am I to quibble with the Powers That Be, right?

Though we had more sunlight in Manhattan, not a lot else changed aesthetically. There were still the cramped quarters, still the roaches, still the elevators reeking of urine, the staircases reeking of urine, the graffiti-strewn hallways reeking of urine, the overflowing incinerator reeking of stale smoke and days-old French toast, the usual scent of dread and poverty.

And there was always the violence. I remember one absurdly hot summer day, leaving the bodega on East Third Street when I came upon two Puerto Rican men on the corner, in each other's faces arguing, clearly high on something. The argument quickly progressed into a fistfight and before I even knew what had happened they had drawn knives. I sat there with the rest of the crowd and watched; it was as if we were all viewers at a sporting event. When the skinny guy dug his blade deep into the chubby guy's stomach the match was over. The crowd dispersed and one man lay dead on the blistering pavement. I learned a valuable lesson that afternoon: Life is fleeting. It can leave any of us at any moment of any day. Maybe you were a part of that crowd, too, Marcus? What did you take from it? It's weird, isn't it? The way we get used to certain things like violence, hostility, being the underdog.

I bet you didn't know my mother gave birth to me when she was sixteen, just a high school student. She dropped out to take care of me and had my sister two years later. My father is not anyone I have a solid memory of. His presence in my life was practically nonexistent, less a shadow than a ghost, really. What my mother saw in him I do not know. Well, he was handsome. This I know because I've seen pictures; black-and-whites of him in his navy uniform. But every man looks good in a uniform, doesn't he?

The only genuine recollection I have of him is a terribly unpleasant one. I was barely six or seven when he came knocking at the apartment door. I was alone, as I often was; my mother had a receptionist job somewhere and rather than pay a babysitter she simply entrusted me to watch my sister all day long while she pulled a nine-to-five. I was good at it, too. Except for this one particular occasion with my father and that one time I nearly burnt down the apartment with candles, nothing ever went wrong.

My father, Jerome Sr., came knocking one afternoon. When I saw the man from the black-and-white pictures staring back at me through the peephole, I just knew my mother would want me to let him in. He was the hero from the war, after all. Only he wasn't really in any war and he wasn't in a uniform anymore. Now he was in tattered clothing, a nervous twitchy energy about him. His face was stretched out and emaciated. At the time, I had no idea what a strung-out druggie was, much less the symptoms of one. When I let him in and he proceeded to tear the apartment apart looking for valuables, I knew something was amiss, so I called my mother at her job.

What occurred after that was the genuinely terrifying part. He, carrying our television in his arms; her accosting him at the front door. He, threatening her. She, threatening him. All that yelling and cursing. And then she pulled that kitchen knife on him—the same large, horror-movie-sized one she used to cut raw chicken pieces—and I thought at that moment I might lose her forever. It seemed to me that he could easily overpower her and use it against her. Thank goodness he just decided to leave with the alarm clock radio as a consolation prize. A couple of years later, when my mother woke me up early one morning to tell me he had been found dead, murdered, I was actually relieved. I would never feel that scared of another human being again. I never even got to see him smile.

Did you know your father at all, Marcus? It's okay to admit it if the answer is no. I used to be ashamed of it, but that was before I realized how common it was for people like us to have no relationships whatsoever with our dads. It's actually a disease in our community. Where we come from, Father's Day is one of those bogus holidays analogous to Arbor Day or Valentine's Day. Or Thanksgiving. Fuck them, fathers who are arrogant enough to leave us their names and nothing more. Fuck them. Fucking fathers. They should be shot, not their blameless children. Perhaps you were thinking of your father when you spotted me walking down that street? Forget I said that. You don't owe me any explanations.

But you should know I had lots of dreams; a whole host of aspirations were floating around in that young imagination of mine. There were things I had planned to accomplish. I was a promising athlete. Little League baseball, school basketball team, weekly football games in Tompkins Square Park. I was successful at all of them. And I was a performer as well. My sister and I often sang together; a little brown Donny and Marie we were. Sure, we only did show tunes from the musicals *Grease* and *The Wiz*, but hey, we had potential. People enjoyed watching us. I was a dancer, too. And I don't just mean my popular disco moves that always ensured I would have female companionship at socials and birthday parties. No, in the fourth grade I was handpicked by Eliot Feld's ballet school to take private weekly lessons at their fine dance studio in midtown Manhattan. Once a week I would get my black tights and white T-shirt on and wear those weird dancer shoes and practice my pliés and my ronds de jambe. Yeah, I was embarrassed to be taking ballet class, but excited as well. That entire world was so fresh and intriguing to me. It was my first glimpse at the way another whole society in New York lived; into a world of whiteness that I had always wondered about.

Right up until our fateful night, I was becoming more involved with drama and musical theater. At Intermediate School 70, I was poised to try out for the next school show and someday attend the famous High School of the Performing Arts. Remember that school from the movie *Fame*? How much fun would that have been? Can you imagine it, Marcus? Can you? My goodness, the promise. The potential. My future would have been so bright I would have had to wear shades!

I could have hated you forever. I should have hated you forever. But that's no way to live a life, is it? Anger can be such a draining force. Maybe you were angry, Marcus. If you were, I understand. Maybe none of those things was ever going to be a possibility for you. Life is not always fair. For people like us it's easy to get mired in resentment and ugly jealousies, isn't it? It's okay, I guess, if every now and then we take things out on one another.

I really just want you to know—I had a life. I had . . . plans, you know? I want you to be aware of that. For all it's worth.

INT. YOUNG BOY'S BEDROOM—NIGHT

DEAN, white, twelve, LAMONT, black, twelve, ERIC, black, twelve, and JEROME, thirteen, all stand around in a circle. Journey's "Don't Stop Believin'" plays in the background on a stereo. SUBTITLE: *THE LUCK OF THE DRAW*

                              DEAN
          Okay, pick a number between one and fifty.
          Go.

                              ERIC
          Twenty-five.

                              DEAN
          Lamont?

                              LAMONT
          Seven.

                              DEAN
          Jerome?

                              JEROME
          Forty-five.

DEAN

It was five. Lamont wins.

Lamont celebrates with Dean while Jerome and Eric express disappointment.

JEROME

Can't we all just stay?

DEAN

Sorry, man, my mom said only one tonight.
She's got a headache.

ERIC

Come on, let's go. It's getting colder out.

JEROME

Shit, my mother's gonna kill me.

three

Have you ever been inside a hospital before, Marcus? My, what fascinating places they are. There is a subtle yet deafening moroseness to those alcohol-perfumed gray halls and white and blue uniformed folk who move about them. Hospitals are like your blandest, least profound nightmare. Being in them stays with you, but not for reasons you would ever care to reflect upon.

Everybody in there wears a mask, surgeons and visitors alike. No one really wants you to see what's going on inside their head. Everybody wants to give the impression that they are being strong and supportive, but in all honesty, they are scared. Terrified even, that possibly someday they could wind up just as miserable and pathetic as you are lying in that bed with your intravenous drip and your stats posted on a wall, your urine dripping pale yellow into a see-through bag at the end of the bed for the entire world to see. It is as if someone had turned your skin inside out and all of your veins and capillaries were on display. That a great number of our fates are inextricably linked to this place is a reality best denied.

Six months, Marcus. *Six fucking months I spent in this place! Half of a year.* And that isn't including the return trips made later for surgeries, infections, therapy sessions. In the blink of an eye I became a member of a club that no one ever volunteers to join: the institutionalized. You know what's odd to me still? Some nearly thirty years later I can still tell you clearly so many of the events there that helped to break me down and pull me up; in vivid detail no less. I still remember the taste of the food, the patterns on the walls, the lines of certain nurses' smiles, the hands of my therapist, the legs of my psychologist, the smell of the liquid soap they gave you to wash up in a basin every morning, the texture and scent of the lotion applied afterward.

I know so many of their names, the good, the bad, and the ugly. Debra, the sexy, voluptuous nurse straight out of *Charlie's Angels*. Donna, the tough-talking, potty-mouthed Italian straight out of a Mafioso casting call. Margie, the sarcastic Latina bitch who gave just as good as she got and wore her white pants so tight you could see her panty line from down the hall.

I can even tell you what my first night was like. From the

stretcher in the emergency room I couldn't even turn my head. All I could do was look straight up at the ceiling. That ceiling, whiter than any cloud I'd ever recalled seeing. The lights in a hospital are oppressively bright. At this moment they were horrid and they were all I had. Anytime someone spoke to me they had to look down at me and into my line of sight. I remember hating that room. I just wanted someone to turn off the lights.

I knew what had happened to me. From the moment my head hit that pavement I knew I had been shot. I could still hear the loud popping noise in my ears; could still see myself falling in slow motion; could still hear the sound of Eric's muffled voice: *Get up, Jerome. Quit joking around.* He sure came around to reality pretty soon. I wonder what it was like for you, Marcus. What did you do right after? Did you go and make a sandwich? Maybe turn on the television to see how the Knicks did that night? Or did you go into your room and cry, painfully aware that you had done something very wrong? Very wrong and very stupid; and now, there was no going back.

I remember my first visitor: my mother. And the shame. The shame, thick like mayonnaise, putrid as a sewer in August. She had wanted me home the night before, but I bargained with her to let me stay out one more night. Hell, it was New Year's Eve. And she had relented. Why did she relent? Weak parenting you think? Hardly. She was losing more and more of these battles with me, as I was getting more persuasive the older I got. The task a single mom faces in attempting to keep her only son in check; most people have no idea. Also, I believe deep down she was happy for me that I had such good friends with whom I wanted to spend so much time. And so that night we made a deal: I could stay over at Dean's but I had to be back home by a reasonable hour the next day. In my mind, there was no "reasonable hour" to return to the Lower East Side. I hated it. My time away from there with my friends had become a refuge, an escape from the dark prison of the Lillian Wald Houses of Avenue D.

But as most long-term prisoners learn, you can leave the confines of the place, but they never really leave you. You will always have the scars. You will always wear the stench of the place like an albatross. You can take the kid out of the neighborhood, but you can't take the neighborhood out of the kid, isn't that what they say? And so it goes, a kid with dreams of grandeur winds up on a stretcher in the corner of a noisy ER trying to see his mother's face as she holds his hand and tells him everything will be just fine, lying to herself and to him because the truth, though still cloudy, is too painful. That truth being that nothing will ever be the same again.

When you are a kid, you know a few things, but the depth of what you don't know is unfathomable. For example, you know that you have a brain, you know that it is somewhere at the top of your head, underneath all your hair, but you don't know jack about the complexities of its mechanics. You have no idea that it is broken up into several different parts that function as a whole. You don't know that there is the cerebral cortex that controls our emotional responses and our language. That there is the cerebellum that coordinates movement and balance or that there is the hypothalamus that helps to regulate your body temperature.

Similarly, you believe that the heart has something to do with feelings of love and affection and that if it is broken it usually leads to sadness and depression. But you know nothing of blood vessels, the circulatory system, the four chambers and the ventricles. What many of us learned about the brain and the heart we probably learned first from the Scarecrow and the Tin Man.

It stands to reason, then, that when I arrived at St. Vincent's Hospital I had no idea of the profound effect that what occurred that first evening of 1982 would have on the remainder of my life. I imagine you didn't, either, Marcus, because if you did I doubt you would have pulled that trigger. For the first few weeks I honestly thought, *Okay, this looks pretty bad, but once these doctors and nurses are all through with me I'll be back out there dancing at birthday parties, trying to dunk the ball like Doctor J or catch the touchdown pass like I was Lynn Swann.* I was clueless as to the realities of what a spinal cord injury was and the permanence of it all. I knew the spine was a sensitive thing because a very pretty classmate of mine with big breasts suffered from scoliosis and had to wear a back brace. Other than that the thought of it never crossed my mind. In my short life I had never even met anyone in a wheelchair.

Now here I lay, staring up at ceilings, crying out for help at all hours of the night. Being fed, washed, poked, prodded, dressed daily (though only in hospital gowns). It took me months to realize that I was still pissing and shitting, just without any control or knowledge of any of it. My goodness, the humiliation of it all, Marcus. The humiliation of it all.

During the first two months it seemed like the visitors would never stop coming. My first visitors after my mother were my closest friends from Westbeth, the housing project in West Greenwich Village where I spent most of my time. It was the morning after my shooting and I was still in shock, but I could clearly recognize their concerned faces at the side of my bed, peering into my eyes, blocking the fluorescent light.

There was the aforementioned Eric, who had to be wondering as I did for so many years—what if things had been different? What if he had been walking on the outside of the sidewalk and I on the inside? What if we hadn't stopped off at Mamie's to play video games for twenty minutes? It was after hours, but the manager was such a gregarious guy and he knew us well, so he opened his locked doors to let us in to play. What if one of us had decided to leave just a little bit earlier that night? What-ifs can kill you if you let them, Marcus. They can eat you up slowly like bone cancer or a flesh-eating bacteria. *What if:* two of the most useless words in the English language. I prefer never to dwell on the what-ifs, but it's so enticing at times.

There was Lamont, my other "brother." Lamont, Eric, and myself were the "three black amigos." We had all met in the fifth grade at Public School 3 in the West Village and became fast friends. We spent numerous nights at one another's apartments, attended sleepaway summer camps together, competed voraciously at video games, traded girlfriends and baseball cards. We had all been walking to school together when we heard the news that John Lennon had been shot and killed. I didn't know much about him except that he sang a very pretty love song about the woman he loved. Lamont's mom played the record endlessly in her room. I couldn't grasp why my homeroom teacher cried at hearing the news of his death. It's kind of ironic now, I guess.

And there was Dean. He lived in Westbeth and it was his house that we were leaving that night after spending the last two nights there. We loved staying over at Dean's because he had his own room complete with a record player, television set, and video game unit. Dean amazed me because he could get away with speaking any way he wanted to his parents. When his mother asked him to clean up his room Dean could say, "Shit, mom, can't you see I've got all this fucking schoolwork? I'll get to it when I can." And Dean's mom would respond calmly, "All right now, honey, no need to get all heated about it. Just get to it when you can."

Incredible. Could you have gotten away with such a thing, Marcus? I know I couldn't have. My mother would have beaten my ass black and blue if I ever dared use foul language with her. It was my friendship with Dean that first opened my eyes to some of the differences between black and white children and their upbringing. I always thought that white kids and their families had things so easy. I saw things only on the surface. I guess that's how most kids see things, but boy did Dean's family teach me a thing or two. I had no idea that beneath all that passive behavior and subtle tension there existed great sadness.

One evening, a year or two after my accident, Dean woke up in the middle of the night and found a note on his bed from his mother. He read it and rushed to his parent's bedroom. From there he and his father rushed to the roof, but it was too late. Dean's mom had already jumped, landing in that same courtyard where for so many years we roller-skated and played Dungeons & Dragons. I can't begin to imagine how deep and all-encompassing her depression must have been. All I could think of was the face of that nice woman who made us peanut butter sandwiches and hot chocolate. Even in my darkest days—and trust me, there were many—I never once thought of suicide as a genuine option. I just couldn't. I'm not a quitter. You helped me realize that, Marcus.

Tamara was another visitor that morning. Tamara had been my homegirl, one I could always depend on for a little carnal therapy should I be feeling restless or horny. Now mind you, we were not even teenagers yet, so our experiences consisted of mostly second-base type stuff, heavy petting, sloppy tongue kissing, but it was fun and exciting. Tamara was quite overdeveloped for a girl her age and a few of us took a go at "exploring" with her in dark stairwells and the closets of friends' apartments.

Behind her back we had degrading terms for her like "Roadkill" and "Too-Easy Tamara"; dumb-ass kid shit. And now here she was, at my bedside, crying and holding my hand while stroking my face. I couldn't feel any of it but it sure felt good to know she was there. I wanted to leave with her. I wanted to go back to that basement laundry room where we had been mischievous together so often and nuzzle up against her full breasts that smelled of sweat and baby powder. The worst part was that I didn't fully understand just why I couldn't.

There was also Lisa, who on the first day of sixth grade

had become the love of my life. I'd walked into homeroom that day and saw the prettiest face I had ever seen. Olive skin, long brown hair, and soft brown eyes; some of my favorite features to this day. I tell you, it was like every cliché ever written that second I laid eyes on Lisa: violins swirled, time stood still, my heart skipped a beat. I immediately took the seat beside hers and for weeks I would pester her in that annoyingly teasing fashion that kids (and at times adults) use to flirt with their romantic interest. Eventually she succumbed to my adolescent charms and we began seeing each other after school. We took the same M14 bus to and from school going east to west in the mornings and then west to east in the afternoons. We would go to school outings and our classmates' birthday parties together. We even went to the movies once with my mother along as chaperone. We laughed uproariously at the sophomoric humor of *Airplane!*

One time especially lingers in my memory, a time when my mother shocked and impressed me. Lisa had come over to my apartment after school, which was against the rules, but my sister was in day care and my mother didn't usually get home from work until five thirty or so. But of course on this particular day, my mother came home early and she found Lisa and me in her bedroom watching television. I expected her to flip out, not just on me but on Lisa, too. Instead she treated Lisa with respect and calmly told me I needed to take her home right away. I just knew when I returned I would get the beating of a lifetime, but to my surprise she never did or said a thing about it again. I bet she just chalked it up to "boys will be boys."

I tell you, Marcus, those early days with Lisa, it was almost like I was meant to love someone, you know? I was good at it. I held her hand, opened doors, bought her little gifts. My knees shook in the elevator the first time I went to pick her up. Don't ever let anyone tell you kids aren't capable of falling in love. Have you ever been in love, Marcus? Has anyone ever loved you? It makes a huge difference in life, doesn't it? I believe a major difference between people who are genuinely happy and people who are generally miserable has to be linked to how much love those people were able to give and receive at an early age. And it doesn't matter how much money you have or how much money your family has. You take a prince living in the Royal Palace or a squatter living in a shantytown, it's the same shit. How they see themselves, how they perceive their self-worth, greatly depends on whether or not someone touched them, someone kissed them on their cheek before going to bed at night, someone hugged them and held them close when they spilled a glass of milk and thought their world was falling apart. These are the experiences that make or break many of us. I hope someone loved you, Marcus. I hope someone still loves you today and that you are able to lavish love on someone as well. You gotta be able to do both. I don't know that anything we do in this world matters more. The main ingredient that got me through this ordeal, both in the hospital and for all the years after, was the love and affection of others. That and my sense of humor pulled me through this dark crevasse and into the sunlight. I can testify to the healing power of unconditional love.

And the funny thing is, I probably have you to thank for it. Now that's fucking irony, if I do say so myself.

EXT. GRASSY LAWN OF A PARK—DAY

JEROME and his uncle, BUTCH, late twenties, are facing each other in a boxer's stance. SUBTITLE: *MANHOOD 101, GHETTO STYLE*

> BUTCH
> Okay, now jab. Jab.

Jerome jabs at Butch's open palms.

> BUTCH
> Harder, harder, Nook. You punch like a pussy.
> Act like you got something.

Jerome hits harder.

> BUTCH
> There you go. There you go. Let me tell you,
> this is the only way you gonna get respect in
> these streets. You hear me? If niggers think

they can push you around, they gonna push
you around. They gonna walk all over your
scrawny black ass. You gotta be a man. And
men use these. You understand me.

Jerome nods, taking in Butch's words.

four

I understand darkness, Marcus. For reasons that I can never explain I have always related to moribund themes. It could just be my nature. Yes, I smile often and people regularly remark how happy I always seem and that is all true; I am one cheerful fellow. But there is a certain blackness about me—not in the dismal sort of way, but I feel like I have an innate disposition to relate to less sunny perspectives. I am drawn to the James Baldwins, the Sylvia Plaths, the Mahlers, the Fellinis, the Chekhovs: artists who embrace life while simultaneously recognizing it is filled with pain and suffering. When I look at paintings I am always drawn to the darker hues in the work. It's why I appreciate van Gogh's *Starry Night*. To me, this painting is clearly expressing that there exist many bright spots in the world, but it is a world mostly filled with blackness.

It is also why as a child I loved *Peanuts* and voraciously read all the comics ever printed in the series. Charlie Brown is the ultimate sufferer, but he still keeps trying to kick the football knowing damned well it will most likely get pulled out from under him. He still throws the pitch well aware it will come back at him, knocking him over in the process. My experience with you exacerbated this proclivity but it in no way created it. My fascination with darkness was there long before you shot me. Ibsen once stated: "Our whole being is nothing but a fight against the dark forces within ourselves." Fascinating theory, no, Marcus?

There were instances in my childhood in which I questioned my behavior: in which I asked myself how I could behave in such a way. These moments almost always involved violence. Once, at my favorite sleepaway camp, located in a small Connecticut town, I went for a walk with a few of my friends. All of us were minority kids soaking up the rich rural beauty that area had to offer, knowing that this was our one chance a year to walk among trees and greenery on empty dirt roads.

On this particular walk, we came upon two white kids, locals, right around our age. They were most likely unaccustomed to seeing so many kids of color in their little town on their little out-of-the-way road and I'm sure we intimidated them because they suddenly picked up their pace and basically ran home. We laughed at them as we continued on our walk, well aware that if the situation were reversed, we probably would have done the same thing.

About half a mile down the road we passed by a house, and who should happen to be out in the yard playing but those same two boys. Being in the secure confines of their yard behind their white-picket fence must have given them a renewed sense of courage. As we walked by the boys proceeded to yell things at us from their porch. The terms *nigger* and *boy* rolled off their tongues with a disarming ease.

This was my first experience of having these terms directed at me in a derogatory fashion. In the hood everyone, black, Latino, even the few white kids there, used the term *nigger* in the same way one would use *dude* or *buddy* or *bro*. There was an unspoken understanding that this was part of the vernacular of our brotherhood. However, these little white kids intended to inflict pain by using these words and their verbal assault had a jarring effect on me. There is a reason why it is solely the male species that is responsible for wars: A little testosterone can be an ugly thing.

I quickly turned to my bunkmate, Hector, a Dominican kid with big ears and a huge Cheshire-cat grin. We all knew that Hector had a switchblade because he was always showing it off at night after the lights went out and our counselors were gone.

"Give me your blade," I said to him, a stern look on my face.

No one questioned my intentions, so strong was my tone. It was as if we were all in agreement that these smart-ass white boys needed to be taught a lesson. Hector instinctively handed me his switchblade and anxiously watched along with the others to see how I would proceed. I had suddenly become the ringleader.

With a skill I must have obtained from watching too many gang-related films I flipped the blade open as if I had done it a hundred times in my life and approached the front gate of the fence. I spoke directly to them, pointing the sharp end of the knife at their faces.

"You like to play games?" I asked, a slight menace in my voice. "Say some shit now, white boy."

The two of them froze. I don't suppose they ever anticipated this type of reaction. I could hear my friends laughing behind me, satisfied with our collective "putting in place" of the boys. There was one of them in particular, the younger one, whose face still haunts me to this day. There was a fear in his eyes at the sight of me, this young black kid with a sharp knife and a threatening tone. That look in his eyes terrified me. I must have appeared monstrous to him. I know that I could have never been a mugger or an abuser of any kind. I couldn't stand the look of fear in my victim's eyes.

After a few seconds of intimidation and posturing I realized that I had been successful in achieving the upper hand

and I put the knife away and walked off with the group. We all giggled and took great joy in the thrill of the incident. The moment quickly gained legendary status as the word spread around camp of my bold, "heroic" action. Its lore was only intensified when later that night a sheriff came to camp looking for me. In his patrol car we had a brief conversation about the event and I assume he chalked it up to juvenile foolishness on both sides, because he simply let me off with a warning to never let such a thing happen again. He didn't even ask to see the knife.

That moment would stay with me forever. I questioned myself repeatedly. Why did I have to pull that knife? Why couldn't I just let it go? Now I was never going to forget the look in those kids' eyes—that sad look of helplessness and genuine fear. I hated myself that I could make another person feel that way. I felt that same feeling in sixth grade when I punched my classmate, Michael Allen, in the face and chipped his tooth for shoving me outside typing class. I hated violence, yet I seemed destined to have it in my life.

These are the types of things one ponders as one lies in a hospital bed for six months unable to move or feel. Thanks to you, Marcus, I was forced to become a most introspective person at a very early age. I started to wonder—maybe this was all some sort of payback for my earlier misdeeds? Perhaps I was being punished for my obvious arrogance? Was I a black Achilles and the Lower East Side my Trojan battle-field?

Perhaps I've gotten a little carried away. Besides, all of that is mere conjecture. Only you know why you shot me, Marcus, and you're not saying much. That secret dies with you.

INT. CHILDREN'S RECREATION ROOM,
HOSPITAL WING—DAY

JEROME sits beside JUDY, a pretty woman in her mid to late thirties. The room is colorfully decorated and littered with toys. They are alone in the room. Judy is showing Jerome a series of diagrams. SUBTITLE: *A PRELUDE TO SELF-DISCOVERY*

JUDY
And what do you think this one looks like?

JEROME
That one looks like a hot fudge sundae.

JUDY
Really? Hungry, are you?

JEROME
You asked me what it looked like and I told you.

JUDY
Fair enough. What does this one look like?

JEROME
That one looks like a hamster ... with a really long tail.

JUDY

Hamster, huh? And what about this one?

JEROME

That one looks like a kid walking down the
street . . . and over here is a guy about to shoot
him in the back.

JUDY

Really?

JEROME

Isn't that what you want me to say?

five

There is a built-in melancholy where hospitals are concerned. For the people residing in them, there is the discomforting sense that time is standing still in your little sphere and the world is moving on without you. The longer you stay in one, the larger that sentiment grows. It is difficult for a resident to get the sense that they are spending their time constructively. The only genuine way I had of telling the time and the day of the week was by noting what television shows were on and when.

Before I came to the hospital, television and I were good friends. I would come home after school and watch repeats of *The Little Rascals*, *Three's Company*, *The Love Boat*, *I Love Lucy*. Maybe two hours of television in a day. Once I became a full-time resident at St. Vincent's, lying in a bed unable to leave it, television became my dearest, most valued, and most dependable friend. I had it on from sunrise to sunset. Now before you judge me too harshly, Marcus, please remember, for the first couple of months I didn't have the strength to even hold a book or a magazine.

In the morning it was news programs, game shows, and reruns of shows like *Little House on the Prairie* and *Fantasy Island*. In the afternoon it was four hours straight of soap operas. I became addicted to the travails of Luke and Laura, Jesse and Angie, the Ryans, the Buchanans, and the Corys. So much time wasted. Then in the late afternoons, it was more reruns, talk shows, and then some evening news and prime-time fare.

Weekends followed a pretty strict schedule as well. Saturdays were full of cartoons and sporting events, followed by every ghetto kid's favorite: Saturday afternoon kung fu films on Channel Five. I still know the theme song by heart. Sundays were always the worst, as aside from football, all of the shows were pretty boring. Especially in the mornings, when most shows seemed to surround church and religious themes.

Everything in a hospital is structured. I've never been to prison, but I imagine life is similar there. You have breakfast, lunch, and dinner at a set time. You can bathe at a set time, and you have to be back in your room by a set time. For six months I lived by this system's rules. It became all I knew.

For the first month or so I was in such a state of shock that I basically sat around receiving visitors and watching television all day. I couldn't even move my arms and had to call a nurse or ask a visitor to change the channel for me. But then I began to receive visits from a team of hospital staff members on a daily basis. They were my rehab team, sent from places unknown with the unified goal of helping me rebuild my life and get me on a road to independence.

At first I found these people extremely annoying, as they always seemed to pop in at inopportune moments (basically, any moment that I was watching television was an inopportune one). Soon, though, I came not only to trust these good-natured folks but to depend on and completely adore them. In a sense they were there to give me my life back. Or, better stated: They were there to lead me down a path on which I would seize my life back. And they succeeded.

My primary care doctor was a young, gregarious redhead named Michael Dempsey. He was kind of the new hotshot doctor on the scene and he had a caustic and naughty sense of humor that jibed well with my own. One could often find us making crude comments about the physical attributes of certain nurses and exactly what it was that made them so attractive. Some of his humor was pretty inappropriate, which made me love him even more. He was just what I needed at that time. And he cared about me deeply. He once told me that I was the closest thing to a son he'd ever had.

My occupational therapist was a plainly attractive young woman with a bright, cherubic face. Her name was Irit Wittenberg and out of everyone I met during my time there, Irit was the most influential person in my becoming the strong, independent person I am today. It's funny, I had a close childhood friend who was Jewish, but religion was such a nonfactor in our childhoods that it never came up during our friendship. Irit was the first person I ever knew who took great pride in her heritage. It was from her that I learned a few Hebrew terms and I jumped at the opportunity to impress her with my multilingual skills, addressing her regularly with a *"Shalom"* and a *"Mah Nishmah."*

Irit had a heart that overflowed with love and devotion toward her job. She was also firm and tough. Her job was to teach me everything all over again, and I do mean everything. Writing, eating, dressing, brushing my teeth, brushing my hair, getting in and out of bed; these were all things I had to learn how to do once more in my new shell. Irit was there for me every step of the way with the determination of a bull and the patience of a saint.

As I mentioned, in the beginning my arms were so weak that nothing came easy to me. I could barely lift my arm above my shoulder. My balance was so lousy and my trunk so weak and unsupportive that if anyone else lifted my arm I would fall to the side. You should have seen me, Marcus. I was like a baby. A baby with a full vocabulary and a sassy attitude. Also, babies will eventually learn to walk and I, of course, never would.

I would get frustrated often. Things like writing, feeding myself, brushing my teeth: These were exceptionally difficult tasks since I could not grasp any object with my fingers. My fingers didn't move. They sat there at the end of my hand like stale sausage links. Irit began to make a set of removable splints for me that I could wear around the room. These splints fit around my hands with Velcro and had slits in them where I could place a pen, a spoon, a comb, a toothbrush. At first I felt silly wearing these big old plastic splints to do seemingly simple things, but after a short time I came to really appreciate the independence they afforded me.

In school, writing had been one of my favorite activities. I knew early on that I was meant to be a creator of fiction, because all through grade school I amused teachers and students alike with short stories I would write on my own. It just came naturally to me, and I thoroughly enjoyed the ritual of sitting down with a pencil and a blank sheet of paper and creating these characters and plots. Now, my handwriting was no different than a child's, barely legible. Due to the lack of control in my arms I had a difficult time writing small enough to fit into the lines of a page. Things like crossing my *t*'s and dotting my *i*'s were suddenly challenging.

To add to my frustration, I had been right-handed for all of my young life, but now I noticed that my left side was stronger than my right, and I had to retrain myself as a southpaw. Dr. Dempsey said this most likely had something to do with the fact that the bullet entered on my left side and that the vibration may have been felt more harshly on the right; some crazy shit like that. Either way, the entry point did have a great deal to do with my mobility. Had you shot me somewhat lower—say around the waist—I probably would have had much greater use of my upper body and a stronger sense of balance. The flip side, of course, is that had you shot me somewhat higher than the neck I could have been a vegetable or in a comatose state. Does one see the cup as half full or half empty? That, my dear Marcus, is the question.

Little did I know that for every hour of occupational therapy you get you also need an hour of physical therapy (PT, which everyone joked stood for "Pain and Torture"). Irit's cohort, my physical therapist, was a freckle-faced young Irishwoman named Cheryl. My time with her was far less pleasant but equally important, as it involved keeping my body in shape. My first few weeks with Cheryl consisted of her stretching my arms and legs in ways that looked uncomfortable (think yoga, but with a second party contorting you) but kept them limber, free of kinks and tightness in the joints. She would also have me work out with a set of light weights that she strapped around my wrists. Similar to Irit, Cheryl had a loving, caring demeanor and though at first I resisted, I couldn't help but come to have affection for her.

There were so many other people that you put me into contact with, Marcus. Besides about a hundred doctors and nurses, there were my roommates. People like Tony, the young Puerto Rican kid with the broken leg who became my partner in crime during the two months that we shared a room. We would watch Saturday kung-fu movies together, play cards, have wheelchair races up and down the hospital halls. Tony's family grew to like me and whenever they came to visit, if they brought something for Tony, they brought something for me as well. His mother came with a big old bucket of Kentucky Fried Chicken, and I got a few pieces, too. And I always shared my gifts with him. Homebaked cookies from my favorite teacher were split with Tony. When Tony finally left to go home I nearly cried; it felt so much like losing a family member.

There was Matt Conroy, the sweet-faced social worker who saw to it that I had all the supplies and adaptations that I needed, both in the hospital and once I left. Matt was interesting because he did so much work behind the scenes for me in terms of making sure my apartment was accessible once I left the hospital, making sure I had school supplies, even hooking me up with social opportunities like summer camps for kids with disabilities. But I rarely ever saw him. He was like the Wizard, pulling all of these strings from behind the curtain. There was Dorothy, the silver-haired teacher in the children's ward whom I had to go see three times a week and who actually gave homework! She really did care so much, that old lady, and I gave her such a hard time. But really, what kid wants to go to school when they are in the hospital? Isn't that really the greatest benefit of being in the hospital when you're a kid—missing school?

There was Judy Silver, my psychologist. My relationship with Judy was a most complex one. I truly resented having to see her because even at that young age I felt similarly to how I feel today: Psychology is a vast and expensive waste of time. Why would anybody want to sit and talk to a stranger for an hour about their feelings when they have friends with whom they could do that? Yes, I know, in the mental health profession one is trained to analyze those feelings and channel them, a thing your average friend ordinarily cannot do, but I have known way too many people who have been in therapy for years upon years. People who have seen very little in terms of actual growth and who, in my opinion, have merely developed a dependence on that analyst. I call it Woody Allen Syndrome. But I digress.

As a thirteen-year-old boy I found it all even sillier. I was unable to take note of the severity of what had happened to me. I was too myopic to consider the effects that such a trauma could potentially have on me down the road and, quite frankly, I didn't really see what talking to this woman was going to do to help my situation. But if there is a God, he or she has a really strong taste for irony and humor. I "tolerated" seeing Judy because she was terribly attractive: a long-legged, brunette looker with light brown eyes that gleamed as she focused on you, and a huge Colgate smile. She had a penchant for wearing high heels and snug-fitting skirts. I don't know about you, Marcus, but growing up in the wonderful multiethnic stew that New York was, I never cared much for race or nationality when it came to women. Give me a great pair of legs, some decent breasts, full lips, a nice smile, and I was there. Count me in.

In the first few weeks I resisted Judy greatly. We had a weekly Wednesday meeting that interfered with my viewing of *All My Children* and that really ticked me off. Sometimes I would even hide from her by going to a different section of the floor and pretending I forgot it was Wednesday. However, Judy always managed to find me and bring me back to our meeting spot, the children's recreation room.

Periodically she administered psychological tests and in my responses I would give her short bursts of answers. Every now and then I would pepper them with a bit of sass.

With that great arrogance that you sometimes find in young people, I truly believed I could outsmart her if I kept on the way I was. But she was good, Judy. I imagine she had dealt with kids a lot brighter and a lot tougher than me in her day. Eventually she wore me down and I came to trust and actually like her.

It's funny, the things that stay with us. Looking back, I can remember with amazing clarity a major talking point that Judy hit upon in one of our sessions. I'm sure I remember it so well because it is an issue that I still deal with to this day. It all started with my favorite game, Scrabble. Judy and I often played board games since it was a painless way to engage me in dialogue. I had spelled the word *legs* and topped it off by stating: "And you've got great ones."

"Really?" Judy said, a tone of surprise in her voice. "I never knew you noticed."

"It's hard not to," I shot back. Even at thirteen, I was a shameless flirt, Marcus.

"Do you think your girlfriends will all have great legs?" she asked.

"I don't know. I don't know if I'm ever gonna have a girl-friend."

"Really? Why wouldn't you have a girlfriend?"

"I don't know. I don't think a lot of girls are looking for a guy like me."

"May I ask, what do you mean when you say, 'a guy like me'?"

"You know what I mean."

"No, I don't. Tell me."

"I just mean, I don't know if girls are gonna like a guy in a wheelchair. Look at me, I can't even feed myself."

Oh, Marcus. Just thinking about this moment now causes a small lump to form in my throat. Even back then I was articulating a terrible insecurity that still plagues not only me, but a great number of persons with disabilities whom I have known throughout my life. It's peculiar, because my disabled friends and I, so many of us are strong, educated, driven, passionate, likable people, but at times we all struggle to get past this one stumbling block: this notion that "I am not good enough. I am not as good as the others. I clearly have less than them as a result of this *slight deficiency.*" It is difficult to explain this shortcoming to a nondisabled person, but I can assure you it exists in so many of my peers.

Every relationship I've ever had since I left the hospital has started out with me feeling this way. This overwhelming concern has caused me to act recklessly more often than I care to admit. At times I find myself needing to sabotage relationships before they ever really get off the ground because I would rather *do* the hurting than be the one eventually *being* hurt. I have ruined a good number of potentially meaningful relationships as a result of this defense mechanism. Despite any strong attributes I may have brought to the relationship, deep down inside I just knew that I was not good enough and that eventually my partner would come around to realizing that, too. I would literally sit around waiting for the "magic" to wear off and to be told, "Listen, Jerry, I really like you, but . . ."

Learning and accepting that I was indeed worthy, that took time. But it inevitably came. And what a marvelously rich lesson that was to learn. I soon learned, somewhat to my surprise, that this feeling of insecurity was not solely the domain of persons with disabilities. I was amazed to find that a lot of "normal" people felt this way as well. From models and sports icons to famous artists and world leaders, insecurity is a condition that grips so many of us. I wonder, Marcus, if perhaps you have ever felt like you weren't good enough for those in your life. Maybe this sense of low self-esteem caused you to fear or to hate, or to mistrust. Maybe it caused you one night to unintentionally commit a dreadful act against another human being.

Well, if that should be the case I just want you to know that I understand. I empathize with you. Self-loathing is one of the worst things that can ever happen to a person, if not indeed *the* worst. I love myself now. I respect myself now. But shit, bro, it was a *lot* of work. And so much of my success was tied to the people at that hospital. That staff at St. Vinny's in so many ways gave me the tools, the courage, and the strength to—for lack of a better phrase—get back on my feet again. There is only one true way you can ever thank a person for this type of act: You can go on to lead a full and meaningful life; share what they have taught you with others. When kindness begets kindness, everybody wins.

EXT. A LAKE IN THE COUNTRY—DAY

JEROME and MIRIAM, a white woman with silver hair, fifties, sit in a canoe, paddling down the lake. After a beat, they stop and just sit there, floating. SUBTITLE: *FAMILY—THE OTHER "F" WORD*

> MIRIAM
> See that, if we just kinda sit here like this the wind will just carry us back to the shore.

> JEROME
> It won't get us home, though.

> MIRIAM
> Well, no, but pretty darn close. Have you decided what you want for dinner tonight?

> JEROME
> Can you please make some more of that lasagna, Miss B?

> MIRIAM
> Of course I can. Dad loves that, too.

> JEROME
> It's so good.

MIRIAM

We were talking last night, how would you like
to come out for Christmas break this year?

JEROME

That would be great. I would love it.

MIRIAM

Good. Good. We love having you here, kiddo.

JEROME

Miss B?

MIRIAM

Yeah, kiddo?

JEROME

Do you think it would be okay for me to stay
with you all and live here?

six

The hospital staff and how close I got to them kind of made me think about family in a whole new light. In a way, those people in the hospital—well, many of them anyway—became family to me because they did what one always assumes a family is supposed to do: They provided unwavering love and support. It doesn't matter that one was Jewish, one was Irish, one was Italian. They were there for me. Wouldn't you agree that is what family is for? What does family mean to you, Marcus? Are you from a large one? A small one? A tight-knit one? Are you able to go back generations and look at your family tree? Perhaps you can trace members of your family to way back when and deduce patterns and notice attributes that help you understand who you are today. I hear about people doing this all the time and it sounds like a great resource to be able to take advantage of such knowledge.

Unfortunately, we McGills have no such opportunity. Or if we do, we sure don't know it or don't care to explore it any further. Mine has never really been a conventional loving family. It seemed we never had that luxury. We have never been a big family, either. Growing up I can scarcely recall a McGill that wasn't in some way screwed up to the point of dysfunction. All of those sitcoms we grew up idolizing—you know, with the Bradys, the Partridges, the Cunninghams, and the Huxtables—to me those were characters from some fantastic and mystical world. I mean, in real life families didn't ever actually sit around a dinner table and eat together, did they?

My time in the hospital and my time recovering at home showed me just how loving and supportive my family could truly be. Aside from my mother, whom I saw practically every day, and my sister, whom I saw on average maybe once a week, the rest of the members of my family I saw maybe once in that six-month time span. And truth be told, that was enough as far as I was concerned. I am convinced that my family was somehow cursed. The analogy I like to use is that us McGills, in our own way, we are like the Republic of South Africa: Each of us is our own little country, wasting away, prideful, but utterly without any real hope. Our suffering is partly of our own doing, but ultimately can be traced to numerous inherited hardships inflicted by fate and humanity.

Tolstoy put it best, I believe, in his opening line of *Anna Karenina:* "Happy families are all alike; every unhappy family is unhappy in its own way." My mother became pregnant with me when she was sixteen. Her mother was none too happy about this and proceeded to throw her out of the house. My grandmother, Evelyn, was a harsh and bitter woman, masterful at the art of alienating everyone within her vicinity. She gave birth to three children and I don't believe any of them could ever honestly say they loved her, nor she them. This is impossible to confirm now because out of the three children my mother is the only living sibling. Both her brothers died before my grandmother passed. But memory serves me well, and my recollection is that no one was ever truly happy in that woman's presence.

When I was very young, my mother would take my sister and me on what seemed to be an endless train ride out to my grandma's apartment in Brooklyn, where she would babysit us with much obvious resentment. She lived in a small, one-bedroom apartment in a ghettofied complex that resembled a prison in lockdown. Her apartment was distinct for a couple of reasons. One, it always seemed dark inside. My grandmother disliked the outdoors greatly and often had the shades pulled closed, even on bright summer days.

Another memorable feature of the apartment was that it always reeked of cigarette smoke and really cheap alcohol, two of my grandmother's favorite pastimes being smoking and drinking. I can barely recall a time when she wasn't already drunk by the time my sister and I arrived, and she usually stayed that way throughout the weekend, with minor instances of early-morning sobriety. I don't know if you have known many alcoholics in your day, Marcus, but there is a certain look and smell that the hard-core ones wear and those close to them don't soon forget. My mother always made me hug my grandmother as soon as we entered her place, and when I got up close to her I could see her eyes were bloodshot and slightly hazy; her scent was a mix of Pall Malls and Thunderbird. And here's a funny fact: When she ran out of either, which occurred at least once a weekend, she would send me to the store to get more. It didn't matter if it was a ten-degree day or a 110-degree night, my ass was going out there to get her some more. And the man at the cash register never blinked an eye when handing me, an eight- or nine-year-old kid, a tiny brown bag loaded with alcohol and cigarettes. That's how things roll in the ghetto.

Interestingly enough, I never really knew my grandfather. Just like my father, I had met him once or twice and only briefly then. I assume he suffered from what I would come to refer to as BMS—Black Male Syndrome. I don't think he was around much in my mother's life, either.

I'm sure that it wasn't so much that my grandmother

didn't love us, or her own children for that matter. Some people just have a hard time expressing anything even close to affection. For reasons I will never know, my grandmother's heart just didn't move in that direction. I would like to give her the benefit of the doubt. I can imagine that growing up in the pre–civil rights era she must have seen some things and experienced certain indignities that no human should ever have to endure. This is the excuse I make for her—the excuse I need to have for her because the truth is, her behavior was deplorable.

I remember very vividly one of my last interactions with my grandmother. She was by my bedside in my hospital room, an extreme rarity, as she almost never left her apartment, much less traveled outside of Brooklyn. And she was sober, a thing I've already noted was rare. She was smiling at me and telling me those same hollow words everyone else would tell me: *Everything's gonna be all right, Jerome. Don't you worry about nothin'.* She was so out of her element that the overall effect was jarring; she seemed like a stranger.

As I mentioned, my mother had two brothers: Uncle Michael and Uncle Butch. These two men were as different as you could possibly get, and the whole time I knew them I never once saw them together in the same setting. Fate had dictated that these two men's lives would take extremely varied paths, but in the end—in one of those great bits of irony that make you almost want to laugh at the cruelty of it—they both died of the same unnatural cause: Both men died suffering and destitute, stricken with AIDS.

Uncle Butch, like his mother, was an addict. His drugs were harder, more destructive. He was strung out on heroin and I'm pretty sure that when all was said and done he was pretty heavily into crack as well. I remember him as a man who had a difficult time stringing two complete sentences together. A man who appeared thinner than he should; who you could clearly see had missing teeth because he smiled a lot; who often looked like he could use a good bath. He had a full and hearty laugh and at the same time he was the kind of guy who gave you the sense that if you left your wallet on the table and walked away for a minute, odds were good it wouldn't be there when you returned.

I don't remember anything about his visits to the hospital, only that they didn't happen often. Maybe twice. Just like his mother he was a creature of Brooklyn. Stepping outside the borough made him feel vulnerable and on edge. When his time came, there was no reason for me to attend his funeral. I didn't know him.

Uncle Michael was a real character, and if I resemble anyone in this family it is probably him. He was a performer, an actor, a musician, a real artiste. He had leading-man good looks and once even appeared in a television commercial, which brought all of us great pride. Uncle Michael was also a homosexual. Know how I learned this? Through a very brief conversation in the kitchen with my mother that went something like this:

"Jerome, what do you think about a man that kisses another man?"

"I don't know. I guess it's okay. As long as he don't try to kiss me."

"Your uncle Michael kisses other men, you know."

"Okay."

The one Thanksgiving that we ever attempted to celebrate as a family was at Michael's apartment in the West Village. He and his partner, a kind Asian man named John, did their best to make it a by-the-books family holiday, but, alas, it wasn't meant to be. When you are a kid you don't really understand what deep-rooted animosities there can possibly be between two siblings. If you have a brother or a sister you know that there are times when they can really piss you off, but it's always the little things. My mother and my uncle Michael really disliked each other, and to this day I am not sure what it was all about. I do have my ideas, though. They were simply two intrinsically different people. Both were highly dramatic, both lived with the scars of supposedly shaming their mother, but the similarities ended there. One was cultured and educated and one was not. They had the same genes, but that didn't make them compatible as friends.

That Thanksgiving Day, my mother and my uncle became involved in a heated argument at the dinner table and she stormed us out of there, cursing as we left. I would see Michael on a few more occasions after I got out of the hospital and unlike with Butch, I actually had a healthy and sincere respect for Michael. I could tell he had a decent heart. He and my mother reconciled before he died and he even came to live with her toward the end, but I'm not so sure I would say they ever really loved each other.

In another great bit of irony, my uncle Michael died at St. Vincent's Hospital, roughly ten years after I checked out of there. He had gone to visit me there during my incarceration, once, maybe twice, but I never went to visit him during his tragically brief stay. It was too much for me to handle. I never attended his funeral, either.

You ever hear that saying, Marcus, "The sins of the father shall be visited unto the sons"? I think it is from the Bible but I'm not really sure. Well, with the case of my sister and myself, one could say, "The sins of the mother and her brother shall be visited unto the children."

My relationship with my sister, Zonnie, younger than me by three years, is one that has always been difficult and strained. I know there was a time as kids when we got along, but once I got older and began to want more independence, things went downhill. Like Michael and my mother, my sister and I are inherently different people. We may have

Me and my sister in happier times.

shared a uterus, but that's where our commonality ends. She has light pancake-toned skin and hazel eyes. I have darker, chocolaty features. As many who knew both of our parents will tell you, she resembles my father. I resemble our mother. If she and I ever had a chance at friendship it was pretty much obliterated the moment you chose to shoot me in the back. Our tenuous relationship was not strong enough to endure this trauma and the subsequent responsibilities and discomfort it would thrust upon us.

I remember when Zonnie would come to the hospital. At the time she was only nine years old, and I am pretty sure she hated it. All of those sick people and the smells and the constant noise and me just lying there the whole time attached to those large machines that beeped constantly. I'm sure she viewed these visits as a great burden to her and I can't say I blame her. When she should have been out playing with her friends she had to be there tagging along with my mother. At a time when she wanted—craved—attention, suddenly everyone's eyes were on me. For a girl who had for years felt like she lived in her older brother's shadow this was a bitter cup of tea to swallow.

Zonnie would go on to attend the same junior high school that I attended and she once told me of the painful process she consistently endured whenever new classes began. When attendance was called and they would get to her name, the teacher would oftentimes look up from his or her book and ask, "Are you related to Jerome McGill at all?" She probably wanted to shoot me herself at those times.

Things should not have ended up the way they did, Marcus. If I have any real resentment for you and the situation you forced me into, it is mainly around this matter of the unnecessary strain it put on my immediate family. I wonder if you have any siblings, younger ones in particular. Don't you feel this natural yearning to take care of them? To make certain that they are safe and protected no matter how strained your relationship? Well, I of course felt this same urge and thanks to you I would never be able to honor those responsibilities that I feel apply to the role of big brother.

After January 1, I would forever feel inadequate in this area. My macho sensibilities had a hard time managing this, coping with this.

I was supposed to be taking the lead in our relationship. I was supposed to be the strong one, the Man of the House. My little sister should never have had to help me get dressed. She should never have had to brush my hair, feed me breakfast, go to the store to buy me Snickers, pizza, or ginger ale. My sister should never have had to wipe my ass. It wasn't supposed to be that way. You screwed up the balance in our relationship, Marcus. It should have been me taking care of her. The equilibrium was rendered askew and neither of us would ever fully recover from it. The same unhealthy fate awaited my mother and me.

My mother is a pretty incredible woman and she probably deserves a medal of some kind for what she went through as a result of my utter disregard for her rules and authority. That night, she knew something was wrong. She would tell me years later that she could just feel it. I was supposed to come home early that afternoon. I chose to stay at Dean's house playing a little longer with my friends. I had hoped that I would get to stay over one more night but Dean's mom decided that two nights in a row with a house of adolescent boys was enough. That's completely understandable. When I called my mother to tell her I was on my way home it was well past the scheduled time we discussed and I knew I would hear it when I got home. This wasn't the first time this had happened.

There were many occasions when I would call my mother from some friend's house, some party, some event, and let her know that I was running late. The way our building was set up there were huge windows in the hallway from which you could see everyone entering the building and many a night did I arrive home late to see my mother's silhouette in that window watching and waiting for me. Sometimes she would yell down to me: "Jerome, you get your black behind up here now!" At these moments it was fairly certain that a good ass whupping was waiting for me once I got upstairs.

However, over the past year I'd gotten taller, stronger, and quicker. I was hitting that period that I'm sure many single moms secretly dread—when they can no longer physically dominate their child. I remember one occasion when I first realized the balance of power was shifting a little in my favor. I had been caught stealing from a local store and the manager called my mother and had her come pick me up. On the way home my mother let me have it verbally and by the familiar tone of her voice I knew the fate that awaited me once we got back to the apartment. Yet when my mother went to hit me with the belt I was able to deftly wrench it from her hand and take off out the door before she could recover in time. I remember smiling as I ran down the stairs, I was so proud of myself.

That evening of January 1, 1982, it was past midnight and I still wasn't home. My mother sat at her spot in the window, camped out, wringing her hands nervously, waiting to see that familiar figure of her son, trudging home guiltily. But as we both know, Marcus, on that night she would not see that figure. No, instead she would receive that phone call that no mother ever wants to receive. Can you imagine what that must have felt like? When she put that phone down and got dressed to go to the hospital? Can you imagine what emotions and thoughts raced through her mind as she got into that taxi, my sleepy sister in tow, and headed to the ER?

I would have to hear about that night for years to come. It was like a tape that my mother played whenever she was angry with me, which was often. In dark moments of our relationship her resentment for me would shine through and the intensity of it was pretty blinding. It most consistently shone whenever she would dress me or feed me or perform whatever menial task that needed to be done that she should never have had to do in the first place had I just obeyed her. I would have to listen to her as she muttered, "I told you to get your ass home that night. But no, you were so smart. Such a fucking smart kid."

And here is the interesting thing, Marcus: The resentment went both ways. Yes, my mother hated me for putting her in this position, but I also had the audacity to hate *her* for putting *me* in that position as well. I had the nerve to hate her for having me too young. For lacking strong parenting skills. For not knowing that if you don't use protection you are bound to become pregnant and raise kids that you could never provide for adequately.

I hated her for raising me in neighborhoods that I was afraid to come home to. I hated her for not being attractive enough to keep a man around. I hated her because whenever I went to my white friends' apartments they all seemed to be living so much better than we did. I hated her for being a statistic: poor, black, single, welfare-recipient mother. How dare she.

Any decent psychologist worth half their paycheck will most likely tell you that in hating my mother for those reasons I was also exhibiting signs of self-loathing; that my animosity toward her most likely mirrored a guilt and shame that I harbored as a result of knowing I had been in the wrong that night. And they would be right. The truth be told my mother did her damnedest to give my sister and me a good, decent, stable, healthy upbringing. She tried her best to get us into decent schools, enroll us in special courses, and see to it that we had unique experiences.

One of the most wonderful things she ever did for us was to send us away with a program called the Fresh Air

Fund. Their mission was to link inner-city kids with families who lived comfortably outside of the city and bring the two together for weeks at a time in the summer to give that inner-city kid the experience of getting away from their environment and embracing a rural community. My goodness, Marcus, to this day I still have these crystal-clear memories and images of my time away with my host family. They are among the most precious of my childhood.

I got to live with a family in upstate New York: Oneonta was the name of the town. I was roughly eight or nine and I remember getting on a bus at the Port Authority with my big army bag and driving along winding country roads for hours. When I finally got off I was warmly welcomed by this white couple, both of them in their fifties or so. They behaved as if they had known me forever. I got into their car (the first time I had ever been in a car) and we drove to their lovely two-story house on the outskirts of town. There I met their two children, a daughter and a son, both in their twenties. All of them treated me with such affection and tenderness I had no choice but to love them right away. Funny thing is, I don't even remember their names now. Let's just call them the Joneses.

The things I got to do with them, Marcus. The Joneses owned a Dairy Queen in town and I got to hang out with them at work and eat all the ice cream I wanted. They also owned a house on the lake and a couple of times a week we would all pile into the car and go out there for the day. We had family barbecues, picnics with neighbors. They would let me take a canoe out on the lake all by myself, no life jacket or nothing. The beauty and serenity of paddling in that canoe all by my lonesome on a warm July morning; all that nature—every city kid should be so blessed to have such an experience. Maybe, Marcus, if you had had that kind of opportunity things could have turned out differently for you; for the both of us really.

I remember crying when that summer ended because I didn't want to leave. I had fallen in love with those white folks and the lifestyle that being with them provided me. I did not want to leave it all behind to return to the nightmare of the inner city. The Joneses were special people, though, with wonderfully open hearts. They assured me they would have me back again and they kept their word. Oneonta became my summer pilgrimage, with the Joneses making all the arrangements. Once, they even brought Zonnie out to join me.

I never really did get to thank them. After you shot me I lost contact with the Joneses. To be honest with you, I don't even know if my mother was able to tell them what happened to me. Like so many of my friendships at the time, I don't know exactly what became of them all. My God, Marcus, when I think of the things you took from me: the precious relationships ruined, fallen to the wayside like ashy remnants of a burnt house. I just want so much to be angry. That would be natural, acceptable even, wouldn't it? But I cannot do that anymore. It takes a lot of energy to stay angry and I want to save that energy for something great. I'm over all of that darkness.

But the scars will remain forever. For several years after the dust settled and I moved away from home, my sister and I barely spoke to each other. Though I was slightly closer to my mother there was also a noticeable void in our relationship and I never felt the need to do much to fill that space. On some level I felt—why bother? I will never be able to make up for the pain I caused, nor will I ever live up to the ideal of the model son every mother wants in her only male child. For making me realize my shortcomings I will always resent that woman. And at the same time I feel cheated by her. She should have been able to provide for me the same glorious life I experienced with the Joneses, shouldn't she?

How sharper than a serpent's tooth it is to have a thankless child! That's Shakespeare, Marcus. Look it up, you son of a bitch.

INT. HOSPITAL CAFETERIA—DAY

DR. DEMPSEY, early thirties, sits alone at a table drinking coffee and reading a paper. DEBRA, a pretty nurse in her twenties, enters and sits across from him. SUBTITLE: *REALITY CHECKS*

>   DEBRA
> Hi.

>   DEMPSEY
> Hi. What a pleasant surprise.

>   DEBRA
> I want to ask you about something.

>   DEMPSEY
> Okay.

>   DEBRA
> Jerome McGill. What's going on with him?

>   DEMPSEY
> I'm sorry . . .

>   DEBRA
> That kid thinks he's just gonna leave this place
> and go back to his normal life. Has no one
> spoken to him about all of this?

DEMPSEY

It's on my agenda.

DEBRA

On your agenda?

DEMPSEY

It's not an easy conversation to have, Nurse
Mitchell.

DEBRA

I don't doubt that, Doctor, but he deserves to
know the truth, don't you think?

seven

They wanted me to cry, Marcus. The staff at the hospital was insistent that there was something wrong with a kid who sheds no tears over such a traumatic event as that which I had recently undergone. Lots of my visitors cried. Even that mean Madame Behn, my sixth-grade French teacher, who made a spectacle out of me in front of the entire class when I was being too talkative one afternoon. She made me cookies and cried at my bedside while holding my hand. It was somewhat disconcerting—the steely Madame Behn weeping for little old me?

The truth is, for the first month or two I had no idea just how serious it all was. I really thought for a while that when it was all over and those doctors and nurses were done with me I would simply return to the life I had once led. It wasn't until I shared this belief with my favorite nurse, Debra, that it became clear to me that life as I had once known it was over and done.

Debra and I had a very comfortable way with each other. She was gorgeous—a blue-eyed, buxom brunette who knew I had an affinity for lovely ladies (boys are so funny; I still remember how she wore her nurse's outfit and how it highlighted her cleavage)—and she was one of those people who truly enjoy their job. It felt like she was meant to be in a place where young people went to heal.

Sometimes Debra would come hang out in my room and watch television with me, especially during the climactic moments of one of our favorite soap operas. We would sit there and yell at the characters, wondering how Nina could marry Steve when it was clearly Cliff she loved. Or why wouldn't Liza stop meddling in the lives of Greg and Jenny. Couldn't she see how right they were for each other?

On this particular afternoon I was discussing my life with Debra and how much I was looking forward to leaving the hospital. Some of my friends had just been visiting and they mentioned that they were heading to the Roxy, one of our favorite spots, a roller rink in Chelsea, later that night. Oh, how many great times I'd had at the Roxy. Skating backward, arms around the waist of a pretty girl, dancing to the music of Donna Summer or the Village People or Blondie. Were you ever a ladies' man, Marcus? I sure was. The chicks dug me!

When my friends came to visit me that afternoon I could feel their anticipation and it was intoxicating. After they left my bedside, skates hanging off their shoulders, I said to Debra, "Man, I can't wait to get out of here and get back to the Roxy. I miss skating so much."

Debra turned to me, a look of calm concern on her face.

"Do you think that when you leave here you're going to go back to your old life, skating and whatnot?"

"Yeah, of course. That's why I can't wait to leave."

She nodded, listening to me, but all the while biting her tongue. At some point she realized she had to speak up.

"Has no one talked to you about what things are going to be like for you once you leave here?"

"Ummm, not really."

"I see."

Debra knew. I'm sure she had seen many cases like mine. Some even worse. I'm sure Debra had experienced death in that hospital. But telling a thirteen-year-old kid that he was never going to walk again for the rest of his life was not part of her job description, and she must have been shocked to realize that after this long, nobody had bothered to break the news to me. I'm almost certain she confronted Dr. Dempsey about it because not long after that he came into my room and pulled the curtain around us, a sign that he wanted a private moment with me.

I was accustomed to daily visits from Dr. Dempsey, but

this one had a different feel to it. Normally he was jovial, even when drawing blood from me. But at that particular moment he seemed tense, as if surrounded by a cloud of some kind. His tone was much more serious. He began by explaining to me the nature and history of spinal cord injuries. He went on to break down the different levels of paralysis as if he were teaching a class on it. He ended by telling me what my level was. I was a C-5/6 quadriplegic. This was based on the entry point of the bullet and where it lodged.

"Historically," he stated plainly, "no one has ever fully recovered from this type of injury. For the rest of your life you will be seated in that wheelchair."

Immediately my mind jumped to a patient I had met the previous month. He was named Leslie and he was introduced to me because Dr. Dempsey wanted me to have some kind of role model and support system. Leslie was in his mid-twenties, a handsome black man who was in a wheelchair. He too had been shot, but his shooting was not a mystery. He had been shot in an attempted robbery. Leslie had been shot very low in the back and thus his paralysis was not as severe as mine. He had full range of mobility in his arms and hands and his balance was perfect. His upper body was greatly developed, giving him broad, appealing shoulders. He looked like a sitting bodybuilder. I had seen

Leslie down in therapy recently and he had begun to use a walker. His upper body was so strong he could pull his legs along as he stood upright.

I mentioned Leslie to Dr. Dempsey and asked if I'd be able to stand up and move just like Leslie did. Dr. Dempsey calmly explained to me that Leslie's injury and my injury were two very distinct kinds. He explained that I was a quadriplegic and Leslie was a paraplegic. For the first time he also explained to me in detail how the bullet was still sitting in my neck and always would remain so. Because it had lodged so close to my spine it would have been danger-ous to remove it, so they just let it stay there. Enough tissue had developed around it that it would always stay firmly in place.

While listening to my good doctor talk, I just sat there emotionless and nodded. I was fascinated and still not grasping the full concept of never being able to walk again. I asked him, "Are there ever any special cases?" He re-sponded that he had not heard of any and he had been in this business a long time. He encouraged me to talk to Judy about it. Talk to Irit about it. Talk to Cheryl about it. But I didn't. I wasn't really ready to discuss it yet, not because it saddened me, but simply because the very concept was too much for my immature brain to grasp in a ten-minute con-versation. The very idea that *I would never walk again* was one I simply could not fathom. After he left I turned the television back on and proceeded with life as I knew it. I did what was most comfortable to me.

It would take about another month or so for the reality of it all to settle in my mind. The great release of emotion that everyone had been expecting and waiting for would come unexpectedly during a therapy session with Irit. She worked tirelessly with me trying to get me to a point where someday I would be totally independent, able to perform every single action on my own without assistance. In the beginning I had numerous doubts that I would ever reach that point. There were times when transferring from my wheelchair to the mat in the therapy room that I would fall and Irit would have to catch me before my face slammed into the floor. Lucky for me she was always there to catch me. She would hold me close to her like a baby in her arms and lift me back up until I was seated upright again.

If there was one thing I definitely feared it was being dependent on my mother and sister for the rest of my life. Judging from my relationship with them, I knew that that scenario would lead to sheer misery for all involved. I wanted so badly to be able to sit up straight with the knowledge that I was my own man. Yet in those early months it didn't seem like my upper body would ever be strong enough to support me. One day while attempting another transfer from wheelchair to bed I lost my balance and fell to my left. Irit propped me back up onto the mat as she'd done a dozen times before. Exasperated, I looked up at her.

"Am I ever gonna be able to do this on my own?" I asked, sounding somewhat desperate. She looked at me, sensing the despair in my voice. Her face softened, but she did not speak. "No, seriously," I continued. "Am I gonna ever be able to do any of this stuff without you helping me?" I needed some kind of reassurance right then and there, but Irit had too much respect for me to give me any kind of false hope.

"I don't know, Jerome. I really can't give you that answer at this moment. These things take time."

That was not the answer I was looking for. Before I knew it, tears were streaming down my face and I was struggling to speak. Irit got up and calmly cleared the room of all the other therapists, who were sitting around doing their paperwork and socializing. After she closed the door she sat back down in front of me, a box of tissues in her hand. Between sniffles I muttered to her. My heart had never felt so thick with anxiety.

"I just don't want to live my life this way."

And then Irit did something I will never forget, not for as long as I live. To this day, whenever I hear someone tell an anti-Semitic joke I cringe a little. I do it because I am thinking of Irit and remembering this moment above all others. At this moment of my greatest vulnerability, Irit started to cry, too. Quiet tears, nowhere near my heaving sobs, but she was crying nonetheless. I wish you could have seen us, Marcus. What an amazing picture life had created at that moment. And just think, if I had left Dean's house an hour earlier or even stayed over one more night, well, odds are that Irit and I would never have met. Yet here we were, sharing one of the most touching moments of my entire life.

"What are you crying about?" I asked her, a smile forming.

"I'm crying because you're my guy, that's why. I want to help you get through this."

I wonder, Marcus, if you've ever known a love like this. Have you ever had someone care about you so much that when you hurt, they hurt? When you need, they need? It is this kind of love that can make all of the difference in the world. And who knows, maybe without this kind of support and affection, maybe without it you do turn into someone cold. Someone without remorse. Someone without a discernible conscience. Maybe you become the kind of person who can point a gun at a child walking down the street and pull the trigger hoping to obliterate a life. And maybe, just maybe, in the long run it is you who needs more support and more understanding than the rest of us. Because maybe, just maybe, growing up deprived of love is the worst thing that can happen to a person.

Maybe he who never cries is doomed to live in a prison of his own heart's making. I want to thank you for putting me in touch with these emotions, Marcus. I really do. To you, I am eternally grateful.

INT. HOSPITAL ROOM—DAY

JEROME sits up in his wheelchair in front of a canvas. He is painting. He wears a splint on his right wrist and a paintbrush has been
fitted into the slot, helping him to move the brush across the
canvas. He goes to dip his brush into one of the cups of paint and
he accidentally knocks the cup over. Red paint splashes onto the
floor. Jerome tries to pick the cup up but he cannot reach it. He
sighs in frustration. SUBTITLE: *WITH ADJUSTMENTS COMES
GROWTH*

eight

I'm not certain that the notion that I would never walk again ever really, truly settled in while I was in the hospital. Yes, I accepted what Dr. Dempsey had told me and worked hard with my rehab team to enter into a new phase, but, again, when you are that age, Marcus, there are some things that your young, undeveloped brain simply cannot work around. There are things one simply cannot fully envision.

I think in a way this inability made things easier for everyone to manage. Who knows, had I accepted that reality early on I might have grown so despondent that my attitude would have been an impediment to my growth. Maybe I would have become a Negative Ned when I needed to be a Positive Pete. Is it possible that the mind works in such an ingenious manner that we take in only what we need to help us move forward and push down a lot of the gunk that will keep us mired in darkness? Surely this would explain how some of us process and ultimately repress early childhood traumas like molestation and child abuse, no?

I don't really have any answers, but what I can tell you is that for the remainder of my time at St. Vincent's I was a generally happy kid, focused on my goals and happy to celebrate every new achievement—and there were a lot of them. I remember in the beginning I had to wear those splints that Irit had made for me to perform all of my tasks. The splints were a workable solution but they were a bit of a nuisance as they were difficult for me to apply myself and I often needed help getting one on.

Then something remarkable happened. One morning I noticed a sharp pain in my left hand. I knew I hadn't done anything to cause such pain to occur and it concerned me some. The discomfort grew over the course of two days to the point where I had to be given painkillers to make it bearable. The medical staff had no explanation for it and took to monitoring my discomfort level. The pain eventually subsided over the course of the week and when it was all gone I had made a brilliant discovery: I could move the fingers in my left hand, to the point where I could grasp and clench things. The fingers in my right hand were still essentially numb but in my left hand I had sudden strength and power. The doctors reasoned that the pain in my hand must have been the nerves coming back to some level of their previous strength or something along those lines.

Either way, I had suddenly gained a much higher level of independence. As long as I used my left hand to perform tasks, I didn't need the splints Irit had made. As a result, I went from being a natural-born righty to being a forced lefty, which was just fine with me. I could even write a letter again. Although at first my handwriting was not as good as it once was, over time and with steady practice I grew to have neat, legible penmanship. I kept waiting and hoping that I would feel a similar pain in my right hand and that eventually I would regain strength and mobility there, but it never happened. For the rest of my life my left side would always be stronger than my right side.

Looking back on this period I think it highlights a wonderful metaphor for the way life works sometimes: I had to go through several days of pain but in the end I came out of it a stronger, more capable person. I have found this to be a fairly consistent pattern.

Other things started to come back to me little by little as well. For the first few months I had needed medical assistance to move my bowels and urinate. Things like suppositories, taken once every other day, and a catheter inserted into my urethra helped me to perform these basic tasks. You can imagine for yourself, Marcus, that this was an area of my life that could very easily cause me a lot of angst and embarrassment depending on how much of it I could or couldn't control.

After a few months I began to notice certain urges coming from my stomach and bladder area. At first I wasn't really sure what they were and what exactly to make of it all. When I told Dr. Dempsey about those sensitivities he started me on a program of monitoring them. I began to pay very close attention to what my body was doing during those times, trying to glean any bit of information that could potentially be helpful to me. It took several months, and there were numerous "hits and misses" but the urges gradually transformed and grew stronger. I learned how to read the signals for what they were and get to the bathroom in time to act on them. Eventually I learned of methods to actually manipulate my body to give me even greater control in that area.

I cannot begin to tell you what an enormous difference this capability made in my overall positive regard for myself and for my self-esteem. I bet you take that ability for granted, don't you, Marcus? Most people do. I bet you simply go when you want, where you want, and are done with it all in a matter of seconds or minutes. But for some people with disabilities, this aspect of life is a major challenge and a source of regular concern and anxiety. I have known people who basically remain reclusive shut-ins because they cannot get this part of their daily existence under control and feel they risk great embarrassment should they venture out into the public world. And so once again I find myself grateful for the "little things" that have made life easier.

Don't get me wrong: Not everything necessarily went my way and not all of the changes that were to occur would be positive ones. One morning I woke up with a horrible fever and I simply could not stop sweating profusely. The doctors treated me with aspirin and antibiotics but I could not stop dripping sweat from my pores. It progressed to the point where several times a day I had to have my hospital gown and my sheets changed as a result of their being drenched in sweat. At the same time I also began experiencing severe chills—right down to my bones, it seemed—and I would spend several days both sweating and shivering in uncontrollable fits of agony.

This horrible cycle lasted for about two weeks and when it finally broke Dr. Dempsey said it was most likely due to the fact that I had acquired an acute adrenal gland disorder, a condition most common to spinal-cord-injured quadriplegics. Basically your adrenal glands control your ability to sweat, and mine were now totally malfunctioning and out of whack. For the rest of my life I would never sweat like your average person does. This can cause major health issues under certain circumstances. For example, when I am out in extreme heat and sunlight, my body is not producing sweat, the body's natural cooling system. Instead that heat and moisture get trapped inside my skin, causing my temperature to rise rapidly. If not treated soon this can lead to heat exhaustion, heatstroke, even death.

To this day I have to be very careful on overly hot and humid days. I must drink fluids and continually cool myself down. As you know, Marcus, our New York summers can be brutal, and there were many occasions when I chose to simply stay indoors all day in July and August rather than risk exposure to the cruel sun. I have had dangerous situations once or twice before when I stayed out in the heat longer than I should have and suddenly found myself feeling faint and disoriented. One of those times I was working in Mexico, and had it not been for the quick reaction of a good friend and colleague, I might have died out in the scorching Guadalajara street. It's a serious condition that I have learned to monitor over the years.

An even more serious, if not the most serious of all the changes to my body developed over a long period of time. Due to the way I lay in bed during those first couple of months when I could not get up, my spinal column began to slowly curve. When I could finally sit up again, my upper body tilted most uncomfortably to the right. If you were looking at me straight on I looked like I was seriously deformed. That's how bad the curve of my scoliosis was. How the doctors did not foresee this or work to stop it I do not know—I think negligence was definitely a part of it—but by the time they actually moved to treat it, it was basically too late. And they greatly botched the first treatment. At first they fitted me in a full-body brace. They molded it around me in bed using hot plaster and I absolutely hated the entire thing. The brace was extremely uncomfortable and prohibitive. I often felt like I was itching underneath it and couldn't scratch anywhere. Imagine if you will, Marcus, that you are forced to wear a shell like a turtle for several months and you already had awfully limited movement to begin with. It drove me nuts.

Then Irit discovered a terribly unfortunate flaw in the brace. She could see that under my left armpit I had developed a large, fleshy raw patch where the brace rubbed against me whenever I leaned that way. Irit had noticed it when she detected a harsh smell emanating from that area and had examined me closely. As it turned out, the area under my arm had grown infected and began oozing a pus-filled secretion. It was absolutely disgusting. The brace was removed immediately and for weeks after I had to take antibiotics that made me nauseous and gave me gut-wrenching cramps and severe diarrhea.

Roughly two years after that, I had my first major surgery ever. It was decided by a team of specialists that the best method to correct my scoliosis would be to graft a steel rod onto my spine, a common procedure for people with weak spinal columns. The rod was named a Harrington rod and the idea was that it would force my spine straight; it was kind of like gluing a toothpick to a rubber band. The surgery was performed after my freshman year in high school, and once again I would have to endure wearing a brace afterward. This brace was even more uncomfortable than the first one. For an entire year I could not remove it, and as a result I was unable to take a shower. I would wash up every morning in the bathroom sink but I still felt insecure. I was sure that everywhere I went people could smell me.

When it was finally removed after a whole year the results were mixed. I still leaned awkwardly to one side but the angle was not as pronounced as it had been. It was the most we could hope for, the best that could be done.

To this day, if you are sitting across from me you probably notice that I don't sit up fully straight. If I have my shirt off you will see that my rib cage protrudes freakishly out of my right side. I guess I'll never be a swimsuit model. When I go through a metal detector the rods set it off. It has made for some amusing moments in airports.

There were other complications, Marcus, but I won't go into a long, dreadful laundry list. Like so many things in my life, the good has outweighed the bad, so I find it unhelpful to dwell on those less enjoyable times. I will say that I envy many of my friends who can state with pride that they have never spent a single day in the hospital. That is a real thing to be proud of. Hospitals are not fun places. I made the most of it all and have great admiration for the dedicated staff who do their best to make one's time there bearable. But I wouldn't wish a hospital stay on my worst enemy.

That being said, when my six months were up and I was faced with the reality of leaving that hospital and moving out into the world on my own, with just my mother and sister as my support, I found myself facing a whole new challenge: fear of the unknown.

INT. HOSPITAL ROOM—DAY

JEROME, wearing sweatpants and a polo shirt, is putting things into a bag. DONNA, a nurse, white, late twenties, enters. SUBTITLE: *CH-CH-CH-CHANGES!*

> DONNA
>
> Hey, look at that handsome fella. How ya
> doing, buddy? You ready to do this?

> JEROME
>
> Yeah.

> DONNA
>
> So, how does it feel?

> JEROME
>
> It feels good. Strange.

> DONNA
>
> I bet. You a little bit nervous?

> JEROME
>
> A lot.

> DONNA
>
> You'll be great, kiddo. You'll see—being home
> will be so much nicer than being cooped up in

here. You about ready? Your mother is down
the hall signing the last of the paperwork.

JEROME

Yeah, I'm ready. I just need a few more minutes.

DONNA

Okay, be quick though. We got another kid
moving in here today. Drunk-driving accident.

DONNA rubs JEROME'S head, then leaves. JEROME looks around
his empty room.

nine

A strange thing happens to you when you spend too much time in the hospital, Marcus. You get used to the place, to the rhythms and pulse of it. The consistency of the monotony sucks you in. You become complacent and somewhat dependent on the routine. You come to crave the womb just a little too much.

In one of my favorite films, *The Shawshank Redemption,* the setting is a prison. One of the characters has been an inmate there for most of his life. When the time eventually comes for his release he becomes very concerned that he won't be able to live in the real world, so accustomed has he grown to life in prison. When he does get liberated he is not quite sure what do with himself. He feels like a stranger in the outside world, like he doesn't belong. Eventually he realizes that he can't make it on the outside and with remarkable calmness, he hangs himself. After six months in the hospital I could easily relate to the angst that character must have felt.

When I had arrived at St. Vincent's that first evening of January there had been snow on the ground and the temperature was down near freezing. I was a novice to the ways of the medical world. I had been to a hospital once, for an ear infection, back when I was in the first grade. I was only there for a few hours, sent home with ear drops and aspirin. How quickly things change. In mere seconds the world as you know it can dissolve away like salt in water. Now that I was poised to leave the hospital everything had changed; there was green in the trees and flowers on bushes. The fresh scent of summer lingered blissfully in the air, calling New Yorkers to shed their clothing and their frustrations. It was June.

Saying good-bye to the staff was one of the hardest parts of leaving. That overworked, sometimes loving, sometimes infuriating group of women and men had successfully steered me through the most difficult transition I would ever make. I owed them so much. Some of them truly were like family. Over the course of six months I had learned little things about them; the things that really matter. I knew what made them laugh. What disgusted them. They shared stories about their lives, their families, their dreams. I had seen many of them cry. In a hospital, the capacity to touch and be touched is so heightened. The caregivers and the cared for go through so much together that at times it is easy to forget where the professional line sits.

Donna, a favored nurse of mine, the Italian Stallion, as I had nicknamed her (I have this annoying habit of nick-naming people I feel close to), accompanied me on my first and only official "night out" from the hospital. About four months into my stay I was invited by I.S. 70 to come back to school for the opening night performance of a play that my dear friend Juliet was starring in. I was nervous about mak-ing the trip back to school as I had literally not been out-doors in several months. Also, the last time I had been in school now seemed like a lifetime ago—I was a whole new person. I felt so much safer about it all when Donna stepped up and agreed to go with me on her night off.

I had a wonderful time at the play. The principal made a special announcement before the curtain rose, asking ev-eryone in the audience to welcome back a very special stu-dent to the school. Of course she was referring to me, Marcus. The audience gave me a huge round of applause. It was as if they all knew me and were all pulling for me. It was rather touching. The show was an entertaining musical comedy, the kind that I might have been in myself had things gone the way I originally planned them. And it was a real trip being back at the school again. All of these people shaking my hand, embracing me, wanting to reconnect with me. When it was all over I felt like Cinderella at the end of the ball because I had to be back at the hospital by midnight. Donna and I stopped off at my favorite pizza joint to get a slice and a soda before heading back to St. Vinny's. We joked afterward about it being our first date.

Anna (Anna Banana as I called her) was a tiny woman—the kind who gave you the impression that if a strong enough wind came along she'd be swept off her feet and into the air. Anna had the distinct honor of being the first woman to ever give me a bath (besides my mother, of course). After months of washing up in bed with a steel basin, lukewarm water, liquid soap, and a washcloth, I remarked to her one morning how nice it would be to take a bath again someday.

Anna took note of that and arranged for me to go down to one of the floors where there was a large, deep whirlpool bathtub. With assistance from two other nurses she lifted my scrawny body up out of the wheelchair and into the awaiting warm bath. She stayed by my side the whole time since my balance was pretty lousy and I didn't feel secure on my own. She held me up with one tiny arm and gave me a full-body wash with the other. I remember feeling so refreshed once I left that tub, like the proverbial new man—refreshed and wanting more.

Deirdre (Big Dee) was the head supervisor down in the Rehabilitation Department. She had her own office and oftentimes before and after my therapy session I could be found in Dee's office just shooting the breeze. Dee was one of those supervoluptuous women with pouty lips and a figure that rivaled Marilyn Monroe's. To say she turned heads when walking down the hall was an understatement.

Dee was a busy woman but she always made time for me. We had chemistry, she and I did, and I liked to think that had we met at a different time and under different circumstances we probably could have had something special. Despite our age difference she entertained me, even flirted with me. She was great fun to hang out with and she never spoke down to me. She treated me like a young man. She even cursed around me, and I loved it. I won't forget the way her face lit up when I came into her office. If she was with someone, she always excused herself from their company to give me a quick peck on the cheek. She made me feel like I was her little man.

There was also Little Mikey, the janitor, who periodically snuck in Reese's Peanut Butter Cups and M&Ms for me. There was Margo, the head nurse of the student nurses. She was always tough on them, sweet with me. There was Rachel, the graveyard-shift nurse who was there for me all of those early nights when I was still in shock, suffering from insomnia, wondering where I was and how I got there. There was Diana (Preggo), who became my Kentucky Fried

Chicken connection. Once every few weeks she picked up a three-piece meal for me along with her own order before coming in. We both craved original recipe.

And of course there was Debra (Fenny). Debra was my favorite nurse of all time, and it was with her that I went through what was probably one of the greatest learning experiences I ever had at that hospital. Even today I still look back on her and the lesson she taught me.

I had this video game, you see—a small but noisy handheld version of Ms. Pac-Man. That game was all the rage back then and someone had given it to me as a gift. This game gave me great pleasure during the day and I brought it with me almost everywhere I went. However, I wasn't allowed to bring it to therapy sessions, so I'd have to leave it in my room. Hospitals can be hectic places filled with human traffic; hundreds of people can pass your room in a day. I came back to my room one afternoon to find that my Ms. Pac-Man game was gone; most likely it had been stolen.

I was furious. Not only had my space been violated by a total stranger, but now I was without my greatest time passer other than the television. I started to act out, blaming the nursing staff for allowing such a horrible thing to happen. I became a real pain in the ass, difficult and distant with them. Even my favorite nurses fell victim to my wrath. One night Debra was giving me my medicine and we got into it. She had jokingly referred to me as a brat and I responded accordingly.

"What do you care anyway?" I spat back at her.

"Excuse me? What did you say?"

"You heard me," I said, louder now. "What do you care about me?"

Debra watched me, an incredulous look on her face. "What, do you think nobody cares about you here, is that it?"

"That's right. You all have your own lives and your own families. I'm just your job, so what do you care if something bad happens to me?"

I was pouting, being overly dramatic in that manipulative way that seems to come naturally to kids. It didn't go over well with Debra.

"How can you sit there and say that? I don't believe you. Look at me. Look at me."

I looked up into her pretty face. Debra had crystal blue eyes. "Do you have any idea how much what happened to you breaks my heart? Do you know that I sometimes leave this place and just go home and lie on the couch, unable to move? Unable to do anything because it just sickens me that you have to be here?"

I had never seen Debra like this before: this serious, this intense. It actually scared me a little. I felt bad for having brought it up, but she was not yet ready to let it go.

"I can't believe you, Jerome. The depression I have gone through—continue to go through—and for you to sit there and tell me I don't care. The other night I went home and my boyfriend wanted to go out and do something fun but I couldn't because I had just left here. Just left you. And I . . . you have no idea the effect your life has had on so many of us."

She walked out of the room. I could hear the pain building in her voice, catching in her throat like a bitter plum, and now she was gone because she didn't want to cry in front of me. She wanted to be strong for me. And so I was left with just her words hanging in the air, thick as tar. I was pretty disappointed with myself. I had managed to upset and offend one of my favorite people in the world. It turns out she did care. According to her they all cared. It had never occurred to me, so myopic was my view of others, so wrapped up was I in my own pathos, that someone else might actually care enough about me to be depressed once they left my bedside. I just assumed that everyone who left me went on to live happy lives and my pain and suffering were things I alone bore. It was comforting to know that someone else cared. It was also the beginning of something. It was the beginning of my looking outside my own little narcissistic world and seeing that other people had things hard, too.

A few minutes later Debra returned with a bag in her hand. She placed it down on my lap.

"Open it," she said in a very demanding tone.

I looked up at her and complied. I knew better than to mess with her anymore. To my surprise there was a brand-new Ms. Pac-Man game in the bag, still in its shiny new box. I looked up at her, not knowing what to say.

"All of us teamed up and pooled our money together to buy you a new one. We were supposed to give it to you at your birthday party next week, but I wanted you to see this now. I wanted you to see just how much people cared about you."

I sat there speechless.

"So now you'll have to promise me that you will at least act surprised when we give it to you next week. Can you do that much?"

I nodded, my shame bubbling up inside of me.

"Good. Then this is our secret. This is not just a job to me, Jerome. Not to any of us. We all love you."

She took the bag back from me and walked out of the room.

That next week the nursing staff threw a surprise party for me in the children's recreation room. When they presented me with a nicely gift-wrapped box and a card I played dumb and smiled a huge, Kool-Aid smile as I tore off the wrapping paper and discovered my new Ms. Pac-Man game. Debra winked at me from the corner of the room.

These moments, these people—they sit quietly in the

deepest, warmest chambers of my heart and soul. Every now and then they peek out and wave hello or tap me on the shoulder as if to say, "Hey, don't forget what took place here." And I know I never will.

For me, one of the most disappointing aspects of the entire experience was that I never really got to fully thank those folks for all they did for me. I wish so much that they knew how much I appreciate everything. It's almost like I feel incomplete as a person never having said these things to them. However, I know that nursing, like teaching, is one of those thankless professions in which the person going into it does so not because they want or need instant gratification. No, they do so because they earnestly care; many of them feel a calling to the work. They have accepted that the path of life is such that the person may not reap the fruits of their experience together until years, maybe decades later. It is selfless work that requires much heart and great inner strength. I can only hope they know how much I love them.

You might ask, Marcus, why I didn't just go back and tell them myself? Well, I tried, let me tell you. Years after my release when I was doing well, living on my own, working and going to college, I would pass by St. Vincent's and pop into the place for a little catching up. But there is a reason why they say you can't go home again. So much had changed in just a few years. Nearly everyone I knew and cared about had moved on to other hospitals or to new phases of their lives.

Debra had gotten married and moved to Denver with her new husband. Dr. Dempsey had started his own private practice in sports medicine. Irit and her husband had moved to Israel. Cheryl had taken a position with a new hospital. Donna and Anna had both decided to stay at home full-time with their children. Little Mikey had died of lung cancer. Margo was still there but she had a new crop of nurses to train and could barely spare a minute to talk to me. Things change, people change. In a hospital there is always an endless stream of new stories being written daily. Old patients, even beloved ones like myself, have to fall by the wayside to make way for the new. I realized quickly that at St. Vincent's Hospital, the book on Jerome McGill had closed long ago.

INT. DRUGSTORE, MANHATTAN—DAY

JEROME, sixteen, and IRENE, white, twenty-six, stroll down an aisle together. SUBTITLE: *THERE'S A FIRST TIME FOR EVERY-THING*

> IRENE
>
> Ah ... here we are.

She removes a box of condoms from the shelf.

> IRENE
>
> Do you have any of these on you?

> JEROME
>
> These? Uh ... no, umm ... I didn't know ...

> IRENE
>
> You *are* planning on coming over tonight, right?

> JEROME
>
> Coming over? To your place?

> IRENE
>
> Yes, to my place. I sure as hell can't afford a hotel. Are you okay with this?

JEROME

Yeah, yeah, of course. I just, uh . . .

IRENE

I thought we discussed this.

JEROME

We did. We did.

IRENE

Good, then let's go.

She walks away with the box in her hand. Jerome catches his breath. He looks like he may be sick.

ten

Do you have any special methods or coping mechanisms that you use for dealing with your anger, Marcus? I'm assuming that you get angry, because not everybody does, you know. Nowadays, I don't ever really get angry anymore. I process things so much better today than I did in the past. But I used to get angry often, and at sometimes unexpected things. I recall one sunny afternoon when Cheryl took me out for an ice cream after our therapy session. It was my first time going outside in months and I was so excited. Because it was a spur-of-the-moment decision, I kept my hospital gown on, and we went across the street to a popular ice cream parlor.

To my surprise, some old classmates of mine were there, and when they approached me to say hello, I was gripped with an unexpected feeling of embarrassment. I suddenly felt that in my hospital gown and with my nappy hair, I wasn't good enough to be among "normal" people. I desperately wanted to be away from them, from the entire public eye. As soon as my friends left, I told Cheryl that we needed to go. Once we were back in the safety of the hospital, I lashed out at her for putting me in that position.

"Why would you let me go out that way?" I tore into her. "Why wouldn't you tell me I looked this way?" My reaction was totally uncalled-for as it truly wasn't her fault, but I couldn't really control my behavior.

At other times it was over even sillier things. If I asked my sister to bring me chocolate chip cookies when she came to visit and she brought oatmeal instead I got mad and ripped into her for being "stupid" and "never listening." I was acting out. Releasing aggression and tension that had been metastasizing for a long time in that frozen body of mine. I tried to "turn that frown upside down" whenever I could help it but it wasn't always easy, you know? I hated myself for getting angry. I'd always believed that anger couldn't get anyone very far in life. I found it a most unappealing trait in others, and I tried to channel all my negative energy into a positive force for myself as well as for those around me.

After leaving the hospital I came up with a few ideas for controlling my anger. The one that worked best for me: trying to focus on the thing that made me upset and then literally visualizing my anger as a bright light in my mind. I would see myself squeezing that amorphous bright light as if it were in a vise and then transforming it into a laser beam of positive energy that traveled through my body and went straight to my heart. I have no idea how I came up with that technique. I probably saw it on a television show somewhere. But it worked for me. To this day I still use that same method.

In the beginning, there seemed to be so many things to be angry about that I didn't know where to focus. Life seemed pretty unfair to me back then, and even today I still struggle with the imbalances of everyday existence. One of the greatest things about living in New York is the range of people you come across on a daily basis. There is no other place quite like it. The variety of classes is incredible. In Manhattan, you can be in a slum one minute then turn a corner and you are suddenly in an upper-class condominium enclave. On the subway, the Wall Street broker sits next to the Forty-third Street hooker.

The disparities we witness can be mind-blowing. I was fortunate in that as a child I had friends in a variety of areas of the city and they were of all races and backgrounds. I had a unique view that I don't think a lot of kids where I grew up had. I saw so much. It didn't escape me that the light brown and dark brown folks where I lived all seemed to dwell in a harsh, overcrowded, dirty community where danger and hostility hovered constantly and the police seemed to harass more than help, but that when I visited my friends in the Village or on the upper digits near Central Park, things literally got sunnier and rosier. The tensions that I faced in the ghetto seemed practically to disappear when I hung out with one of my best friends, an Italian kid, who lived in trendy Gramercy Park.

It is easy to find oneself pondering what exactly the differences between all of these people are. Did some of them really work that much harder than others in order to be successful, or were they just lucky, born into good fortune? And why is it that so many hardworking, law-abiding, good-hearted people get trampled on in this world and so many immoral, unconscionable scofflaws skate by living an apparent life of luxury? It is these types of questions—surrounding the basic unfairness of it all—that cause me the most conflict in terms of believing in any "higher power."

Before you shot me, Marcus, I never thought much about religion. I feel fortunate today that my mother was not a churchgoer when we were children and made no effort to force any theological beliefs on us. That gave me the freedom to look at a variety of religious theories and eventually come to my own conclusions without my own family's faith interfering. I guess the closest term that defines my belief is *agnostic*. I don't have any true respect for the popular organized religions that dominate our culture; to me they all seem riddled with hypocrisy. But I wonder about the existence of a higher power. I'm hopeful that one exists, yet I have serious doubts. It's nothing that I lose sleep over; it just seems to come up every now and then. Especially that question of unfairness. I feel like I have seen too much darkness to believe in any higher power. And I'm not just talking about my own life: All one has to do is read the newspaper on a regular basis to get an idea of what a cruel and ugly place this world can be. But I'll be honest with you, Marcus: Though I've come to appreciate and honor the man I am today, I do believe that a lot of my doubt is attributable to you and what happened between us. There is just so much I still don't know and there is always that eternal issue of what could have been. I know that I gained so much, but at the same time I feel I lost so much as well. It's difficult to reconcile what happened to me with the existence of a higher power.

For example, I think I would have made a great father. I love kids, and I feel that as someone who never knew his own father, I would have overcompensated with my own kids. I know that I would have been an extremely strong presence in their lives. Not overwhelming, mind you, but a powerful force and an unwavering source of strength. Of course, none of this is certain. For all I know I could have been a serial impregnator, one of those guys who have six baby mammas and don't have money to support any of them. Who knows what could have been? There's really no way to know for sure, but I can tell you this—the McGill name is going to end with me. Uncle Michael was gay and had no kids. Uncle Butch had three daughters. I am the last male McGill that I know of who is alive from my family and I don't foresee any kids in my future. Not that I haven't had my chances.

Relationships have always been a struggle for me. Although I have always been attracted to women and always will be, it doesn't change the fact that with my level of spinal cord injury, the ability to "perform" is always questionable. Right before you shot me, I was beginning to notice things. Little hairs were growing in places. When making out with a girl, or, hell, even when looking at a pretty woman, I noticed a stiffness occurring. I remember my mother once trying, very uncomfortably, to have "that talk" with me about the birds and the bees. It was shortly after she had noticed how enamored I was with Lisa. She was so humorous and cute in her inability to articulate just what she was trying to say. It must be hard for a single mom to have this conversation with her male child. That's really a father's job, isn't it?

"Now, Jerome," she'd said, the both of us taking a seat at the kitchen table, cementing the seriousness of the conversation. "I just want you to know that what you're feeling is

natural ... Do you sometimes feel ... like ... a hard-
ness ... down there?"

I don't remember just how that talk ended, but I do
know that most of what I learned, I learned on the street.
That's the way it usually is in the ghetto. You know what I
mean, don't you, Marcus? I'm sure you had a similar school-
ing.

In the hospital I never really thought about sex that
much, despite the fact that there were so many lovely
women around—nurses, doctors, therapists, psychologists,
cleaning women. I was only thirteen when I got there, four-
teen when I left. I still had to go through that awkward
phase of hating girls, didn't I? (That phase never came, by
the way.)

It wasn't until about junior high school that I really
began to wonder about girls and how I was going to manage
the sticky yet curious swamp that was sexual intimacy with
a disability. I had to attend a new school, one that was specifically set up for kids with disabilities. This school was on
the Upper West Side. The first floor was all students with
numerous disabilities and challenges. The second and third
floors were for the "normal" kids. My fellow disabled students marveled at my ability to mingle in both crowds—our
crew and the "upstairs kids," as we referred to those "normal" kids. While at this school I became involved with two

girls. One had a disability and one didn't. I knew guys in my neighborhood who were already sexually active at my age but I had no idea how to broach that subject with them. I had no one to talk about sex with. I would have to play it by ear.

Penny was the girlfriend with the disability. She was a very pretty young woman from the West Indies. She had spina bifida, a birth defect that manifests itself in numerous ways. In her case, she actually had more mobility than I did. She wore leg braces and could walk around pretty easily with them. Alicia was my other girlfriend, an "upstairs" girl. She was pretty in that nerdy librarian kind of way. She and I were both involved in student government and we would spend one afternoon a week holding hands and kissing while we made memos and posters for school events.

And yes, Marcus, before you ask, I did see both of them at the same time. It was a little tricky at first, but I managed it.

These relationships were simple in the sense that I only saw these young women at school and thus never had the opportunity to feel any kind of pressure to "act." At that age and in that space, making out and petting were quite sufficient. Neither of us wanted or expected things to go any further.

It was in high school that things got a little more complicated. One of my high school girlfriends, Dawn, wanted to go to a movie with me one Saturday afternoon. We made plans for her to pick me up from my apartment (I wasn't so comfortable getting around the city on my own just yet) and from there we would walk over to the movie theater together.

Normally my mother or my sister would be hanging around the apartment doing something, but on this particular Saturday both were out for the afternoon. When Dawn arrived we found ourselves in the excitable position of having the whole place to ourselves. We sat on the couch to watch a little television and before long heavy making out ensued. I'm pretty sure that if it were you, Marcus, or a lot of other guy friends that I knew, the next scene would take place in the bedroom with the lusty couple "knocking boots," "making the beast with two backs," and all those other great euphemisms. But that wasn't going to happen with me. You see, I was terrified. Terrified of failure in this oh so crucial sphere of Maledom. Terrified that I would be so mediocre or even worse, such a disappointment, that no woman would ever want to see me afterward. That in fact, she would tell all of her friends just how horrible I was and I would become a laughingstock: Limpdick Jerry.

We grew up in a macho culture, you and I did, Marcus. Our mentors were men like Muhammad Ali, Shaft, Wilt Chamberlain, and Marvin Gaye. You could never picture one of those guys having to stop in the middle of getting it on because they couldn't get it up, now could you? I was pretty aware of my ability range. I had made mental notes on numerous occasions of what it took to arouse me. Late at night while watching cable television I had masturbated to a few of the light porn shows that came on after midnight and I knew the effort it entailed to get me excited. Bottom line, I couldn't get aroused by images and feelings like your average Joe. With my level of spinal cord injury, that ability was gone. To get an erection I would need physical stimulation, and to get that physical stimulation my partner would have to do some extra work. This would require a decent level of communication between us and, sadly, I just didn't know how to make that conversation happen. It was that conversation that truly terrified me so. In my mind, no Real Man would ever have to have that conversation with his woman. A Real Man would just put on some Stevie Wonder, take her by the hand, lead her into the bedroom, and get to business. She would come out an hour later thoroughly pleased and hungry for more. This was how my sixteen-year-old brain imagined the world of intimacy worked. And from where I sat I was never going to be a true player in this world because my manhood was questionable at best.

And so, that Saturday afternoon, with Dawn and me on the couch, getting hot and heavy, her blouse off, my hand up her skirt, her warm mouth sucking on my earlobe, the body heat melting our skin like butter on warm leather, the minute she moved to undo my pants I panicked and stopped, coming up with the first lie I could muster: "My mom should be home any minute. We should stop here." I would never allow myself to even attempt to take it further because I was so afraid of what could happen if I discovered I was unable to be a man.

Can you imagine the shame I felt, Marcus? Dawn was ready, willing, and able right there that afternoon, and I just didn't have what it took to follow through on my end of the deal. As she buttoned her blouse, fixed her skirt, and re-touched her makeup, I just looked away, knowing that on some level she must have already thought so much less of me.

But if you're lucky, Marcus—and I think luck is some-thing we are all capable of attaining—you grow from these experiences and at some point you are able to overcome your anxieties and live a more healthy and productive life. Oftentimes it takes help from an outside source. I got this help from so many people in my sphere. The courage and strength people recognize in me would not be so evident had it not been for my friends and their loving support. In this particular area, that of sexuality and intimacy, the earli-est and most inspiring help came from a foreigner from New Jersey, nearly ten years my senior. Her name was Irene.

As a child before the accident, I had always attended sleepaway camp every summer. It was a great thing to be able to get out of the city for a while, and it also provided a great relief to my mother. I was concerned that after my accident I would no longer be able to enjoy such opportunities, but my social worker, Matt, found a camp in New Jersey that was specifically designed for children with disabilities. I was ecstatic when he told me he had signed me up for a two-week session.

I made tons of friends at that camp, some I'm still close to today, but the most meaningful friendship was with Irene, a counselor. Irene was the kind of full-figured woman I was always drawn to and with her crimson pigtails, freckles, and plain face, she kind of resembled Pippi Longstocking; but with sex appeal . . . and an Australian accent. That summer the camp had hired many counselors from abroad as part of an international exchange work-study program and Irene was intriguing and fascinating to all of us city kids because the closest we had ever come to an Australian was Olivia Newton John's character, Sandy, in *Grease*.

Irene and I had similar senses of humor and we spent a good deal of down time joking around and enjoying each other's company. At first it was all very innocent and friendly, mild flirting between a precocious fifteen-year-old and a somewhat sophomoric twenty-five-year-old, but that next summer, my final summer there, when I was sixteen, the relationship took a turn for the glorious. Irene was granted a work visa and she stayed in the States for another two years, landing a job as a caregiver at a school for disabled children in New Jersey.

During the school year Irene and I would write to each other about once a month. We would share many things about our lives, including romantic endeavors. Periodically I would ask her advice on a situation and she was always supportive and complimentary. She made it clear to me that I was attractive—a catch, as they say—and that I need never be bashful or fearful of approaching a young woman. I had struggled with my confidence early on, you see. I bet you never struggled with confidence, did you, Marcus? Or if you did, you could easily shrug it off like so many brothers in the hood seemed to do.

When I returned to camp that summer, I had begun to enjoy writing again and I was trying my hand at poetry. After lunch at the camp we had rest hour and I took that time to write Irene a poem nearly every day. Marcus, let me give you a bit of advice—a poem can be a lovely calling card. There are not many women out there who can resist being even mildly attracted to the man who takes the time to put his emotions and his feelings for her down on paper. And it's all the better if he has some talent working a metaphor, a simile, and splashing a dash of imagery here and there. Poetry, when original and sincere, can be a wonderful assistant in massaging a woman's heart.

Irene had never had a guy write her poetry before, and

after a few days of consistently receiving my heartfelt missives she started to look forward to her daily poem. When one day I didn't write her one, she came looking for it. Her face actually registered disappointment when I told her I had been too busy to write her. It was at that moment that I knew I was on to something. I could see our chemistry changing, intensifying. I was simultaneously scared and excited. Irene and I were actually falling in love right before my eyes.

Have you ever been in love, Marcus? I mean really been in love? The kind where when that person touches you, your heart beats so fast that you think it just might leap out of your chest and take off into the night sky like a liberated butterfly? My God, it's a wondrous, exhilarating thing. I hope for your sake that you have felt it, bro. No one should ever go without having felt it just once. I began to have these moments of felicity with Irene. We had to be extremely discreet because what was happening between us was very much against the camp policies and could have gotten her fired, but we took our chances nonetheless.

While attending a late-night bonfire and in the safety of darkness, Irene would gently stroke my neck or I would softly rub her knee or thigh. Any chance for us to connect was seized upon. We found a secluded spot out in the woods where I took to reading my poem to her aloud as she held me close, holding my hand. I had never truly been with a woman before, and she knew it. We had talked about it a couple of times and the idea of being my first lover excited her. We made a plan for once camp ended. She would come to the city and pick me up and we would spend time together the way we wanted to, without fear, uninhibited.

When that day arrived I was a ball of nervous energy, but Irene was wonderful. She came to the apartment, charmed my mother, and swept me out of there. We caught an afternoon showing of *Purple Rain* and then had an early dinner in Times Square. We were able to kiss, cuddle, and hold each other tight in the big city and I was on top of the world for it. All at once I felt like we were just the same as all of those other lovers one sees in Central Park, walking down Fifth Avenue, making out on some corner in Greenwich Village. Yes, I was black and she was white. Yes, I was in a wheelchair and she was fully able-bodied. Yes, there was a good ten years separating us. But that's part of the beauty of New York—nobody really gives a damn. Diversity is New York's middle name. We looked happy and we weren't hurting anyone. We were bathed in that same bright light of contentedness and it made me feel like a whole person, a feeling I rarely ever had.

I could have gone home that night and lived off the euphoric high of those feelings for days to come, but Irene had even greater plans. As we drove toward the Lincoln Tunnel I suddenly realized where we were going and I was scared she could hear my heart beating through my chest, it was so deafening to me. That moment every young person fantasizes about, worries over, had seen in countless teen movies and read about in a number of young adult novels—that moment had arrived for me.

Oh, Marcus, growing up as we did I had all these ideas about sex and about lovemaking; preconceived notions about a man's role and what makes for a satisfying sexual experience. I had this idea that it was a man's job to get it all right. That it was so important for me to be able to get in there and drive my manliness home. That without me and my savage thrusts and grunts the job was never going to get done properly; the mission never completed. At first these notions worked against me and made my anxiety such that I was not going to be able to function, period, much less be a dynamic sex machine.

And here is where having a patient, experienced lover came in handy. I am so grateful that my first time was with someone like Irene: someone who had already had several lovers prior to me and didn't need me to take control. Because I simply was not ready to be in that role just yet. I needed a guiding, compassionate hand and Irene was all that and more. The conversation that I needed to have with so many women before, all at once came easily now. There, in Irene's queen-sized bed, she quizzed me on everything from just where I had sensation to what felt good to me to what positions would I prefer to explore. In those early moments in her bedroom, I was terribly awkward and the first two times we were not successful. But persistence pays off, don't ever let anyone tell you differently.

That night was my first real lesson in what it means to be a lover; I became aware of several of the limitless sources of passion and pleasure the human body holds. I learned that a man is not measured by the width of his thighs, the number of times he can thrust his pelvis back and forth, the quantity of his ejaculate, nor the size of his cock. I realized just how sweet the flesh can be. I also realized just how powerful the spirit can be. I learned how to listen to and read a murmur in the dark. I discovered the benefits that follow a softly placed kiss, a firmly placed stroke in the most tender of spaces, the elation that can come when two people are fully aware, focused in on every shudder, every blink of an eye, every breath their lover releases. This didn't all happen in one night, and in fact, it is still happening to this day, but I have learned that lovers can be like musicians playing in a grand orchestra: When they are in tune and they take the time to hit all the right notes, they can create a symphony most magical, most eternal, and practically incandescent.

The mind is such a potent tool, Marcus. We can achieve so much if we simply learn how to harness our thoughts and energies; how to funnel them into a broader, grander ocean. Life is so full of ups and downs that sometimes it is a great challenge just to remember this, but damn it, I want to. I want to always keep this mentality at the forefront of my thinking and if I can help others see their potential along the way, well then that would be a beautiful thing, too. The lessons you helped me learn are too precious to keep to myself.

eleven

It's been thirty years now, Marcus—thirty long and glorious years since that night of nights when you and I came together in our ever so eventful nonmeeting. In the very beginning, the anniversary used to mean something to me. For the first five or six years after, I would get melancholy and depressed as it drew near. It would start right around Christmas and last straight through to the first day or two of the new year. I would kind of mope around in my sullen state, pretending that the holiday season didn't matter and acting like I was above it all. In essence, I was merely masking my pain.

Then at some point I had an epiphany. It was somewhere around my freshman or sophomore year in college. Things were going quite well for me: I was living on campus at Fordham University, getting a fantastic education that I wasn't paying a dime for (the result of numerous scholar-ships), I had a wonderful group of friends, I was involved in theater, acting, writing, journalism at school; I had nothing to complain about. That Christmas break I went to Los Angeles to visit a dear friend of mine and somewhere (I think it was while watching a sunset on Santa Monica beach) it hit me: Happiness is a thing I can control if I put my mind to it. It is *my* perspective and how *I* choose to see my life that is really going to make the difference at the end of the day.

Yes, something lousy had happened to me not long ago, and in a perfect world that would not have occurred. But look at me. Look in the mirror. I'm still here and I'm still thriving. I began to ask myself, *What the hell right do you have to feel sorry for yourself when schoolchildren are being shot in the back in Soweto and AIDS is decimating an entire section of our population, not to mention what it's doing abroad?* I began to do the simple act of crunching the num-bers, comparing the things I had to the things I didn't have. The results were blindingly clear. I *had* a hell of a lot. I had no reason to go on playing Vinny the Victim. It was time for me to step up and appreciate.

I had my mind, my heart, my soul. I had a sense of humor, a strong personality. I loved people and people loved me. The positives so greatly outweighed the negatives. All at once it occurred to me: I could give this event with

you, Marcus, dominion over me and my feelings about myself. I could look at January 1 as that infamous day that forever wrecked my life, *or* I could recognize the beauty that is
still very much a part of my everyday life despite an unexpected inconvenience, and I could honor that beauty.

My God, Marcus, there is so much beauty in life. If you
look closely, you can see a hundred acts of kindness and
love on a daily basis. Especially in New York, the greatest
city in the world. Once I summed it up in my mind in that
manner, the decision to see the light in all that had occurred
in my life immediately became a no-brainer. I started a new
phase. I began to celebrate the outcome of my existence.
From then on, on every January 1, I would take an opportunity to buy myself something special; a gift to commemo-
rate our anniversary. One year it was a nice new shirt,
another year it was a necklace, one year I took myself out to
dinner at a fancy restaurant, one year I flew myself to London for some sightseeing and theater. Whatever I did, I saw
to it that I didn't allow myself to get bummed thinking
about what I possibly had lost. I was going to focus on what
I had and could still someday have. To this day I still celebrate that day. Our very own holiday. In my dark humor I
like to refer to it as Shot In Back Day.

Last summer I did something really special, Marcus.
Last summer after decades of ignoring that location (our

The block where I took my last steps.

spot?), I made a choice and returned to it. I went back to the scene of the crime if you will—I returned to Seventh Street and Avenue C, the place where it all began for us.

My family had moved away from that neighborhood, you see. While I lay in the hospital, my mother was working hard to get us a new place. She was determined that I would never have to go back to that area. To her it was an ugly, filthy place that had shamed and forsaken us all, and she thought it best if none of us ever had to breathe Lower East Side air again. I can tell you, I was most grateful to her for this. Aside from the mental aspect, physically the building we lived in was a nightmare for someone in a wheelchair. Tiny elevators that were always breaking; thick, heavy lobby doors; a tiny bathroom. No, it would have never worked—a change was necessary.

The new apartment we wound up at in Chelsea was a welcome fresh start. It wasn't that the apartment was any nicer (it wasn't) or that the area was so much safer and cleaner (just slightly), but it was what it was: a new beginning. There were no ghosts walking the streets. To all of our neighbors I was just a kid in a wheelchair, not that poor kid who used to play ball in the neighborhood but who screwed around, got shot in the back, and was paralyzed for life. I was so relieved not to have to deal with that condescending shit on a regular basis.

Again, our new building wasn't perfect. There were three huge steps to get into it, and for years I had to be lifted up and down them every time I came and went until the building department eventually installed a ramp. Funny thing was, no one bothered to take any measurements or consult me; the ramp was too steep and I still needed help getting in and out of the building. The elevators broke often as well. Sometimes I would hang out in the lobby for hours until they were fixed. Alterations had to be made to the bathroom so my wheelchair could fit; walls had to be knocked down and a sliding door replaced the standard door. All in all, things worked out just fine. But despite all the adjust-

Graduation from Fordham University. A very proud day for me; I am the first McGill to graduate from college.

ments, I was happy to leave for college in the Bronx and get away from there as soon as I had the chance.

At Fordham University I pursued an English literature degree but I also spent a great deal of time working on my theater skills, both in acting and writing. I joined a company for people with disabilities (the National Theatre Workshop of the Handicapped) based in Manhattan and I had to attend classes and rehearsals in the city a few nights a week. The trip into Manhattan from the Bronx was about an hour each way and though it took a toll on my studies, I did it because the experience of working with that theater company was such a positive one. There, at NTWH, I met older, more experienced people who had lived with their disabilities much longer than I had lived with mine and I found many mentors among them. For the first time I saw people with disabilities who were leading successful, "normal" lives. They worked, had children, drove cars, things I had wondered if I would ever do. They became a great source of support and advice for me.

I also joined a theater company that worked with children in the impoverished Hell's Kitchen area of Manhattan, called the 52nd Street Project. There I was able to write and act in plays with kids who all reminded me a lot of myself when I was their age. They were all mostly black and Hispanic kids and my years with them were precious and unforgettable. After I graduated from Fordham the 52nd Street Project hired me full-time to be their production manager, and after many happy years there I got restless and moved away from New York altogether. I had been a New Yorker my entire life and I was anxious to see what the rest of the country had to offer. I had grown weary of bitterly cold winters and snowstorms that rendered me immobile and I decided I would give the West Coast a try. I still live out west today, but I have had numerous opportunities to visit New York since I left. Last summer was the first time I made the conscious decision to eradicate the last of my demons and set foot—or wheel, in my case—back in the old neighborhood.

Me and one of the kids from the 52nd Street Project performing a play out-doors.

I wonder if you are still there. My goodness how things have changed! Back then in the early 1980s, the whole place had an eerie, burnt-out feeling to it. At night when walking down the streets you felt as if you were walking through an old abandoned Hollywood film set of a World War II ghetto in Berlin, buildings ravaged by heavy artillery, the stench of dreams deferred floating in the air. Crack cocaine was just beginning to rear its ugly head and the residents were beginning to show the wear and tear of it.

This past summer, as I rolled up the street and looked around at the old place, I didn't see one location that resembled the old one that we knew so well—the ghetto of our youth. Sitting right there on the spot where I fell, the last spot I ever stood up in, I was surprised to be surrounded by trendy, "hip" bars and cafés, restaurants where people of all races sat outside and ate under large umbrellas while being waited on—like one might see on a quaint Parisian street. There were pretty murals on the walls and a healthy, busy energy to the hood. Clearly at some point the real estate world discovered they had a gold mine on the Lower East Side and realized that if they built it up, yuppies, baby boomers, and trust funders would come. And come they did. Gentrification had long since obliterated any signs of the land we once knew. It was fascinating to behold. An overwhelming amount of peach skin now dominated an area where only brown had dared to roam.

It wasn't so much that I had felt a strong need to avoid that neighborhood as it was that I just honestly never saw the benefit in going back there. I didn't see until then how retracing my steps and visiting old haunts would do me any good. But sitting there on that warm July afternoon, I felt a sense of pride swell up inside me. I wasn't sure why I felt that way. It wasn't like what I was doing was so monumental or exceptionally brave, was it? I looked over at a young white couple a few feet away from me holding each other close while their poodle relieved himself on a tree. I had to smile. They had no idea that not too long ago, before they were born even, a young boy fell to the ground right there, gasping for breath, afraid he was going to die in that very spot.

I looked up at the window, the one from which Eric's mom was yelling down to us. She was telling us to hold on, that she had just called the ambulance and they were on their way. I couldn't turn my head but I could hear her voice. I could hear all of them talking around me: strangers and Eric alike. They were saying things like "Is he alive?" and "Don't move him."

Now, decades later, I found myself wondering if you were there somewhere. Again, I smiled mischievously at the notion that maybe, just maybe you were sitting in your window right then looking down at that guy in the wheelchair. Perhaps you were bored and there was a commercial break in your television show, so you chose to look out the window. You probably didn't give me a second thought. I've changed infinitely since that night.

For one thing, I don't go by the name Jerome anymore. At some point, shortly after I left the hospital, I realized that deep in my heart I no longer felt like Jerome. Jerome was a young boy who had stellar dance moves. He loved Rick James and the Jackson Five. Jerome was a second baseman on his Little League baseball team. He dreamt of being another Reggie Jackson or Willie Randolph. Jerome played touch football in Tompkins Square Park. He dreamt of being a wide receiver for the New York Jets. Jerome had a mean three-point shot; he practiced it often on the glass-strewn courts of the Lillian Wald housing project. He dreamt of being another Darryl Dawkins. Jerome was an incorrigible flirt at the roller-skating rink. He taught Vicky Higgins how to skate backward, sneaking kisses as he did so. Jerome had just started taking a musical theater class. He was singing "Maria" with his teacher. He had a decent voice, but he struggled mightily at reading music.

Jerome was many things that after the accident I felt I no longer was. When I got to junior high school that September and my new teacher called out my name, I corrected her and said, "It's actually Jerry." She made the correction in her book and that was that. Out with the old, in with the new.

I pissed off a few of my old friends. One of my more sensitive friends was a lovely girl named Zuri, who secretly harbored a crush on me. She had been hanging out with us that New Year's night but she had left early because she was bored at our insistence on playing video games for several hours straight. When she heard me refer to myself as Jerry she flipped out.

"Stop calling yourself that. Jerry is the name of some nerdy white guy. You're not Jerry. You're still Jerome."

I ignored her, though. She didn't understand. None of them did. After I got out of the hospital I found I didn't have much to say to any of my "pre–St. Vincent" friends. We couldn't really relate to one another anymore. They always seemed to be pitying me and I always seemed to be envying them. It didn't take long for us to go our separate ways. I've been Jerry ever since.

I still love movies. I always have and always will, I'm afraid. I often go alone to the cinema. To me there is something so calming, so peaceful, so therapeutic about sitting in a dark movie theater and watching a splendid piece of filmmaking, especially if it is one of epic, lyrical quality with great scenic locales like, say, *Out of Africa, The English Patient,* or *Dreams.* After the credits roll and the lights come up, I sometimes experience a brief sadness knowing that I have to enter the real world again.

For years I tried diligently to get a job in the filmmaking business, even living in Los Angeles for a time while pursuing it. It's a tough market to crack. In many ways the film world is like an old boys' club. You have to have a combination of great connections and even greater luck to get just a peek at the menu. I seem to have neither of those things, but I keep trying because I am stubborn. I'm not a quitter and I haven't got a whole hell of a lot else to do. It's in my blood. I have written numerous screenplays and even shot two short films, but the powers that be in Hollywood don't think there is a huge market for stories about people with disabilities, despite all of the Oscar-winning portrayals that have come from actors playing disabled characters.

This is one thing I hope to change: people's perceptions

A short film that I wrote, acted in, produced, and directed. Try as I could to market it I couldn't get anyone to take me seriously. A love story about a black guy in a wheelchair is not considered "bankable" in the film business. It still stands as one of my proudest achievements.

about people with disabilities. It's actually one of the reasons why I feel perhaps it was my destiny to become a person with a disability. I know I said I'm not a very religious person, but I do believe there has got to be a reason for everything; some reason why we are where we are in life. Some purpose we are all meant to serve. There have been times when I have felt extremely fortunate to be in a wheelchair. Like it was the perfect position for me to be in at that moment.

For example, after college I got a temporary part-time gig teaching theater arts and playwriting to a classroom full of children with disabilities at a high school in Queens. These children had all been sequestered from their able-bodied counterparts and basically pushed to the side of a small wing in the school building. When I arrived on my first day of class I asked them all what issues they wanted to write about. Many of the students voiced frustration at being alienated from their able-bodied peers and made to feel like second-class citizens at the school. I saw great dramatic potential in the topic and jumped on it. I loved their honesty and emotion and proposed that we write a series of one-act plays around the theme of alienation.

I then went to the principal and told her what we were working on. I told her that I thought it would be a great idea if the students could present these works to their peers in the hopes that it could get a dialogue going and enrich the experience of both the able-bodied and the disabled community at the school. She agreed with me. I was given a small technical crew to lead and a couple of months later we staged the shows in a very professional manner and performed them at a school-wide assembly. They were a huge success. The response was even greater than I had hoped for. Shortly after the shows, inclusion programs were instituted to bring the groups together. My students with disabilities felt a sense of elation at the idea that their voices were being heard and respected. At my going-away party several of them thanked me for "helping them feel like they belonged." It was a priceless experience.

A person without a disability would have had a hard time carrying out that project with the same effectiveness with which I did it. The whole reason why the students felt comfortable opening up to me was that they looked at me and saw me as one of them; someone they could honestly confide in because they could easily assume I had been down their same road. I was honored that they entrusted me with such a responsibility.

This type of role—that of a mentor for persons with disabilities—is one I have played often and I savor it. I honestly feel that it is one of the reasons why being in a wheelchair seems appropriate for me, as strange as that may sound.

Once I left New York I got another temporary job working for a company dedicated to taking young people with disabilities on international exchanges. It was a mission that was dear to my heart because I'd always been enamored with traveling abroad. Sadly, I'd been dissuaded from doing so while in college because the study abroad advocate at my school didn't think it was a good idea for a guy in a wheelchair to be anywhere near Europe. This form of ignorance and discrimination would not be tolerated today, but back then, unfortunately, it was par for the course.

However, this company I worked for—founded by a

woman with polio—jumped at the chance to give people with disabilities the experience of travel and it was an honor to be a part of numerous trips. I was a group leader and I would visit the host country before we went. My job was mainly to pick out accessible sites and meet with the people we would live with while there. I did my best to ensure that my participants—a group with varying degrees of disabilities—would have their individual needs addressed during our time in that country. Once again I found myself in the wonderful role of mentor to young disabled people.

Have you ever had the opportunity to travel outside the country, Marcus? I hope for your sake you have. You can learn so much and grow so much as a person from seeing how another culture lives their lives. Here is just a small sample of the marvelous globe-trotting pleasures I have had:

- Sipped rich coffee in a Costa Rican rain forest.
- Cruised along the Champs Elysées after stopping at the Louvre and viewing the *Mona Lisa.*
- Sang a duet at a karaoke bar in downtown Tokyo with my lovely host mother, who had an affinity for Disney songs.
- Performed at a vintage theater in England with a wonderful acting troupe of disabled performers.
- Driven about one hundred miles an hour on the exciting, yet scary, autobahn in Germany.

Me and a group of my students in San Jose, Costa Rica. It is my belief that I was always meant to work with young people.

- Marched in a disability rights protest on the streets of Mexico.
- Played chess with a blind Russian man on the banks of Lake Baikal.
- Represented the United States in a table tennis tournament at a beach resort in Siberia.
- Visited the childhood home of Wolfgang Amadeus Mozart in Salzburg, Austria.

- Drank fine red wine while viewing the bold architecture of Antoni Gaudi in Barcelona.
- Taught English language lessons to elementary school kids in San Jose, Costa Rica.
- Made out with a paramour under the clouds in London's Hyde Park.

This is just a small taste, Marcus. There is so much more I still have to add to my itinerary. I have never been to Africa or Australia, Italy or Iceland, Greece or Guam, but I plan to. I promise you, I will never allow this wheelchair to be an impediment to achieving my goals. I would be shaming the both of us if I did.

I have to say that being in this "situation" has given me some amusing interactions with the public. I have been fortunate to know a great many people with disabilities—having belonged to numerous organizations in my day—and so many of our stories are similar. Some eerily identical. When you have an obvious physical impairment, for some strange reason people think they can just approach you about anything. Like on a public city bus someone will just ask you at the top of their voice, "What happened to put you in that chair?" or "Why don't you just get up and walk?" At times it is humorous, at times upsetting.

Once, in Manhattan, I got into a cab to go to an appointment. The cabdriver was obviously of Middle Eastern descent and after I got settled in beside him in the front seat (it's easier to get into the front seat than the back) he turned to me and said in his heavy accent: "So, let me ahsk you sumding. You cannot be widd woomahn, right?"

"Excuse me?" I asked, slightly incredulous.

"You—you cannot be widd woomahn dis way, right?"

I was actually amused. These kinds of things always amused me.

"Yeah, I can be with women. Of course!"

"Your payniss, id can ged steef den, yes?"

"Yes, my penis can get stiff. Why would you think it couldn't?"

"I dohn know. I am juss ahskink, mon." There was a brief pause as he mulled it over in his brain. Clearly I'd thrown him a curveball. A cripple who could get it up! Unfathomable! "Steel, id eez a pity, really."

"What's that?" I asked, just baiting trouble.

"Well, clearly you cannot do eet doggie style."

What do you make of that, Marcus? And he was sincere in his sorrow for me, so pathetic was I because I could not do it "doggie style." At the end of the ride he patted my shoulder condescendingly and refused to take my money. I suppose he imagined I would need it for hookers.

Which leads to another thing—money. I can't tell you how many times I've been offered it by strangers. I'll be hanging out on the street waiting for a bus and someone will walk by and just hand me a bill. I'll be eating a hot dog in the park and someone will just hand me a bill. Whether or not I take the money depends on what mood I'm in. I can recall two separate occasions where I have been outside enjoying a cup of coffee in the sun and someone has walked by and dropped coins in my cup.

Possibly the best story involves my brief encounter with a gentleman on Fifth Avenue and Fifty-seventh Street. While waiting at a red light to cross the busy intersection at the height of rush hour on a glorious spring day, I was approached by a very distinguished-looking white male. He was wearing a noticeably expensive suit and carrying a fancy leather briefcase.

"Good afternoon, young man," he said, extending his hand.

"Good afternoon," I said, shaking his hand.

"You look like you could use a new wheelchair."

"Oh, this one is just fine."

"No really, how much do they cost?"

"They're pretty pricey."

"How much?" he continued, reaching into his jacket pocket and producing a checkbook and a pen.

"Ummm, really, I'm comfortable with this one."

He clicked his pen with authority. "I'm offering to buy you a new wheelchair, young man. Do you want it or not?"

"Really, I'm okay, sir. Thank you, though."

"Suit yourself," he said, putting his checkbook and pen back in his pocket and moving along with the changing of the light.

You can't make this stuff up. People think they can just invade your space and deny you your privacy, and in addition they feel that you should be grateful to them for doing so. I have a theory on this: Most people—and I blame the media for this—look at people with disabilities as not wholly human. On some level they view them as objects to be pitied. These people who offer me money, new wheelchairs, or ask me probing questions about my personal life in taxicabs and buses, they think I should feel fortunate and blessed that *anyone* even wants to converse with me.

Here in America we actually have it easy. I have been to countries where people with disabilities have told me that they are so looked down upon by society that it is incredibly oppressive. The unemployment rates for them are staggeringly high. In many countries in Latin America, Asia, Africa, and Europe, people with disabilities are not expected to be active, contributing members of society. They are expected to stay at home and either receive government assistance or beg in the streets. It's that simple. Here in America we at least have the Americans with Disabilities Act, which is intended to stop this type of discrimination at all levels. But of course it has its imperfections. Changing people's attitudes and perceptions is seriously challenging work.

Personally, I feel like I am up for this challenge of being a person with a disability and I have had many a wonderful experience in this role, but it is hard, damned hard, Marcus. And I will be the first to tell you, it is not for everyone. I have had tons of disabled friends over the years and the misconception that we are all strong, inspirational beacons of hope is an immense fallacy perpetrated by and subsisting on images in the media; Jerry Lewis telethons and Easter Seals poster children are probably the greatest offenders.

Trust me, I know a lot of bitter, angry, depressed, and self-destructive people with disabilities. People who suffer greatly from self-esteem issues. People who see life as somehow having robbed them of something they were never fully able to enjoy. These people wallow in their self-pity, attempting to heal their pain with addictive behavior. And I'm not judging or condemning them—like I said, this life *is not easy.* Let me quickly run down just a few of the hardships:

- Bathrooms. Do you have any idea what a drag it is to need to use the restroom and not have one that can accommodate a wheelchair in the vicinity? My goodness! This might be the thing most taken for granted by the able-bodied community. I had a job once in Manhattan where there wasn't an accessible bathroom in the entire skyscraper. Whenever I had to use the bathroom I had to go to a building across the street. Aside from the time-consuming aspect of it, you can imagine what a pain this was in the winter months and during inclement weather. Another quick story on this theme: Once I was on a date with a beautiful woman I had just met at a conference. We went to a lovely restaurant where the romance was high and our attraction grew more intense by the minute. But after a few glasses of merlot I was seized by the urge to use the bathroom and this restaurant was unequipped to handle me. I spent the rest of the night greatly distracted by my bladder and eventually lost out on a fantastic opportunity for a one-night stand (and maybe more?) with an utterly sumptuous woman. And don't get me started on the impossibility of airplane bathrooms.

• Housing. I have found myself looking for apartments on numerous occasions in numerous states and once even in Europe. It is always a bit of a challenge, as there are certain nonnegotiable features in a domicile that I require. Wide bathroom door, room to move around in once inside that bathroom, no stairs to enter the building, low countertops, a kitchen I can navigate, an elevator I can fit in. Finding all these things in a place can be terribly frustrating. In times of desperation I have had to make do with what I had, especially when living abroad, but the difficulties in achieving satisfaction in this area should never be underestimated.

- Employment. Quite possibly the most frustrating of all the challenges. I don't want to sound pretentious or smug, but I went to a revered Jesuit university and got a bachelor's degree in English literature. I went on to get a master's degree in education. I wear a suit well and can be articulate and engaging. I should be an appealing candidate to prospective employers. But to this day I still have to deal with discrimination in the job field. Not too long ago I would have faced prejudice because of my skin color, but nowadays it's that "other" attribute that can hold me back. I cannot tell you how many interviews I have gone on where I knew from the look on that interviewer's face the minute I wheeled into their office that I was not going to get that job. Many people still feel uncomfortable and awkward around people with disabilities and they prejudge and size them up in an instant. I have been rejected for jobs that I could do in my sleep. It doesn't matter that I dress up nice, speak well, and present myself impeccably. A large part of the population refuses to see a person with a disability as a whole person. This *has* to change. The injustice of it all is shameful. I plan to work my ass off to be an integral part of that transformation.

I have achieved so much, Marcus. So much. And though I am ending this book now, I still believe in my heart of hearts that I have two or three more books left in me. There is so much more work I need to do. My story is not half over. But this part of it is—this need to reach out to you, to touch you. I have satisfied that part of me. Writing to you has been like reaching deep into my soul and unlocking a door, and once walking through that door, opening a window and letting sunlight and warm air into a cold room.

For years I lived with fear, wondering if I could ever truly love myself. Would the world be able to love someone like me—someone so different yet so the same? To my great relief the answer was a resounding "Yes!" I am thankful.

For years if I heard a loud pop I would begin to shiver, an immediate reaction I never could rationalize. It went away with time. To this day I still periodically have troubling dreams. In them I am chased through the streets by a gunman who in the end shoots me in the back. At first they were disturbing and when I awoke I struggled to go back to sleep for several hours. Nowadays I am wholly unaffected by them. I just assume my subconscious is working this shit out on its own. For years I fantasized about finding you, meeting you, torturing you, forcing you to address me and apologize to me for what you did to me—what you turned me into.

But all that darkness is gone now. The day I knew my life was going to be just fine was the day I realized that I didn't need to hate you. You know why? Because it's easy to hate someone, and I don't want to take the easy way out. Anger is the default emotion for so many of us, and I don't want to give anger that kind of power. No, the way you win this battle is to stand your ground and pronounce to that black abyss:

Yeah, you tried to take me out. Tried to beat me down, turn me into a statistic. But you know what? I'M NOT GOING OUT LIKE THAT! Is that your best shot? 'Cause I've taken it. Literally. And I'm still here. And I'm going to continue to prosper and thrive. What do you think of them apples?

I need to embrace you just as I need to embrace the person I became. You and I, Marcus, we were following the script of our lives. I may have been a bit player in yours, but you were a major player in mine. And I respect that. All the same, I want to make one thing perfectly clear in this whole scenario. With all this gratitude and appreciation for who I am and the person I became, it doesn't change one integral, salient fact in this matter and that is simply this: What you did was wrong. Inarguably, unequivocally improper.

You just don't have the right, regardless of what you've been through, to walk into someone else's life and inflict unimaginable pain and hardship on them and the people they love. That is a right that you *do not* have. What you did to me, Marcus, was selfish and cruel. It was an ugly act of cowardice that is beneath all of us as human beings. And remember, what you did didn't just affect me. No, it affected hundreds of people, both close to me and maybe less intimately related but who nevertheless felt the ripples of that bullet piercing my spine. In the end, what you did surely enriched the lives of some, but it inevitably diminished the lives of others.

Two instances jump out at me as I tell you this. One involves Erica, my pretty blond childhood friend who lived on the Upper East Side. Erica and I met at that summer camp in Connecticut. Roughly ten years old, we became tight friends, calling each other daily on the phone while our parents were at work, spending summer days after camp was over just hanging out at the park in her neighborhood or going to the local swimming pool together. She dropped off the face of the earth after I went to the hospital.

About ten years later, while rolling past Lincoln Center, I passed by an attractive blond woman sipping a soda in front of the fountain. We both stopped in our tracks at the sight of each other as a memory stirred. It was Erica, all grown up and lovely. We embraced and she started to cry. We spent about an hour catching up. I was shocked to learn from Erica that my accident had had a profound effect on her childhood. For several years after my shooting, she would see a child therapist because she was so hurt and confused by what happened to me. She had even come to see me once in the hospital, but she had a panic attack when she got to my room and saw me hooked up to all those machines. She could never bring herself to come back.

And then there was Dalton, my childhood friend, and one of the few white kids on the Lower East Side. Dalton and I often took the bus to school together. I spent many a weekend hanging out with Dalton and his younger sister, playing games and being kids together. After my shooting, Dalton's parents were so upset that they promptly moved out of that neighborhood and never looked back. Decades later Dalton would write a book about his experience growing up there and I would be featured prominently in it.

But these are just two stories. There are countless others that I will never know. I truly hope, Marcus, that in your quietest moments you have thought about this. I hope you have meditated on it, agonized over it, and ultimately come to terms with it. I hope that you have felt guilt and shame, but I also hope that you have learned how to let go of it all and forgive yourself. I honestly believe that I have.

Someday I would be honored to meet you; to look you in the eyes and shake your hand. My instinct tells me that will most likely never happen. And I'm okay with that, too. It isn't absolutely necessary, because here is the thing, Marcus: At some point in life all of us will be in the *wrong place at the wrong time*. At some moment we will all be "assaulted" in one way or another. For a select few, it will come early in their development; for others it will come later in life. But rest assured—it will come. No one escapes the night.

And when that moment arrives it won't matter what your assailant's face looked like; whether you saw it coming or you were caught completely off guard. No, at the end of the day all that will matter is that under the dense weight of all that occurred, when all was said and done, you had the strength and the fortitude to lift yourself up, open the door, and step out into the light.

EXT. STREET CORNER—DAY

JEROME sits in his wheelchair looking around him, marveling at how things have changed. An OLDER BLACK MAN, tired-looking, walks up beside him, smoking a cigarette. JEROME turns to him. SUBTITLE: *EPILOGUE*

> JEROME
> How you doing?

> OLDER MAN
> Fine. You?

> JEROME
> Chilling.

FADE TO BLACK.

acknowledgments

I am most grateful to my mother, Doreen, and my sister, Zonnie. Though we struggled mightily and things weren't often pretty, these are two strong women who have achieved a lot under extremely difficult circumstances. My mother, in particular, I owe so much to because I honestly believe I inherited her strength.

To Lorrie Moore: So inspired was I by her beautiful, eloquent prose that I reached out to her only in the hope that she would know how much I appreciated the gift she possessed. She took it upon herself to heap praise upon this memoir and it made all the difference. Her support changed my life.

To my resplendent editor at Spiegel & Grau, Hana Landes, who chased me down through the tree-lined streets of Portland, Oregon, to bring my book to the greater public.

Hana's belief in my story was just what I needed to make a dream come true for me and I will forever be in her debt. My entire team at Spiegel & Grau were such a pleasure to work with—they made the transition from small-time writer to larger-time writer a smooth one.

To Shalom Auslander—this cynical bastard was there to provide me with his wonderful, darkly-humorous take on the literary world and he introduced me to my agent, the dedicated Lydia Wills. I thank them both for believing in me.

To Dalton Conley, one of my oldest friends—he has known me since I went by "Jerome." His own writings on our unique childhood have been a subtle and moving inspiration to me.

To brother Rick Curry, S.J., the founder of the National Theater Workshop of the Handicapped, who pushed me to do something I never really thought I'd care for—get a college education. It really was worth it! Sort of.

To Willie Reale, the founder of the 52nd Street Project, and Carol Ochs, the executive director. They gave me my first job out of college, even sought me out. The experiences I had with their theater company laid the foundation for numerous successes in my life.

And last, but definitely not least, to my hospital staff at the now-shuttered (tragically so) St. Vincent's Hospital in

Manhattan. I never got to thank any of you but your love and comfort took me from a dark place to a light place. How do you thank someone for that? I guess you try to pass that kindness on. Transfer what you learned from them into so-called wisdom. Maybe you write a book.

JERRY McGILL is a writer and artist. He received a BA in English literature from Fordham University in the Bronx and his master's in education from Pacific University in Oregon.

Jerry McGill is available for select readings and lectures. To inquire about a possible appearance, please contact the Random House Speakers Bureau at 212-572-2013 or rhspeakers@randomhouse.com.

about the type

This book was set in Minion, a 1990 Adobe Originals typeface by Robert Slimbach. It is inspired by classical, old style typefaces of the late Renaissance, a period of elegant, beautiful, and highly readable type designs. Created primarily for text setting, Minion combines the aesthetic and functional qualities that make text type highly readable with the versatility of digital technology.